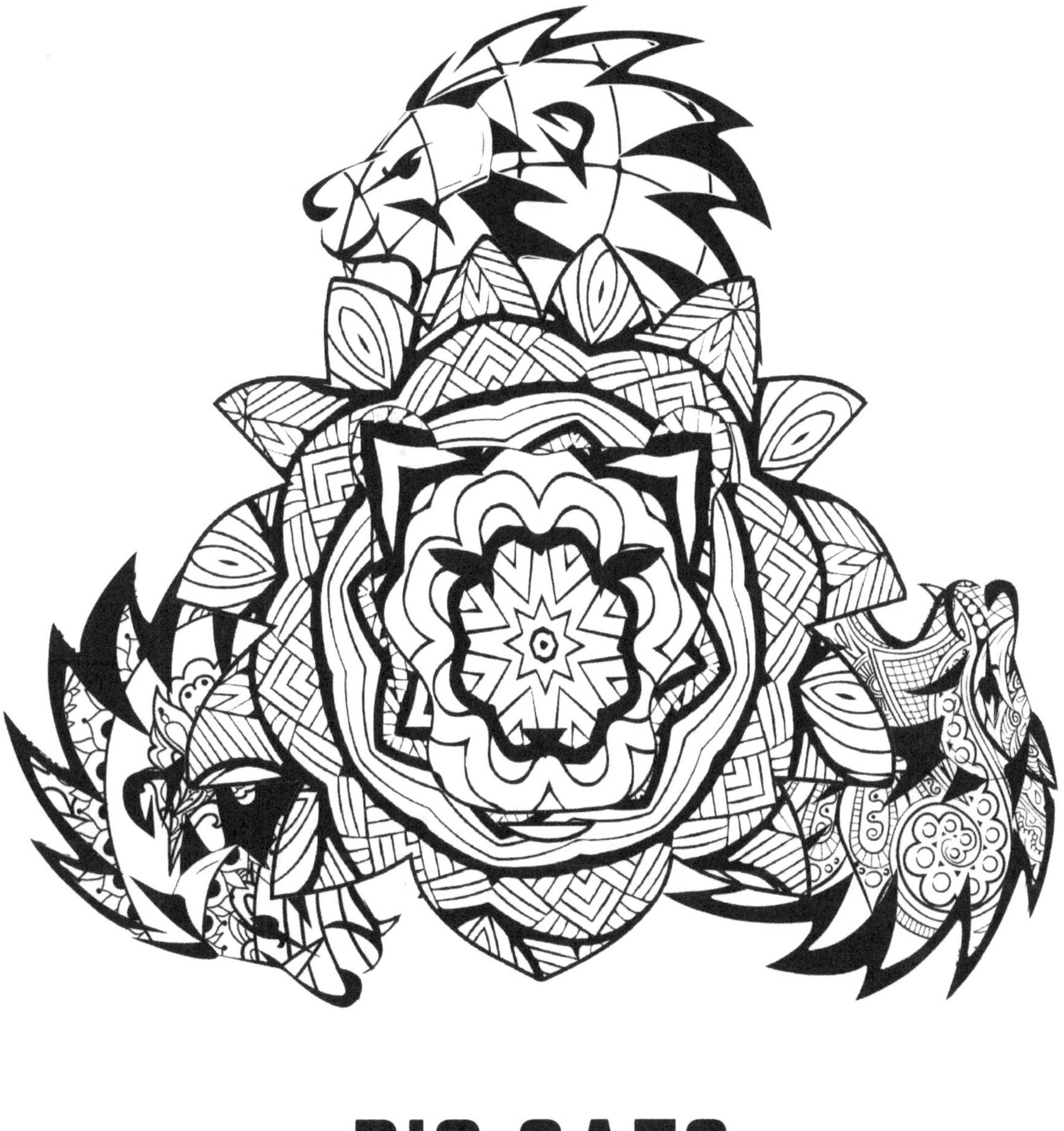

BIG CATS

COLOURING BOOK

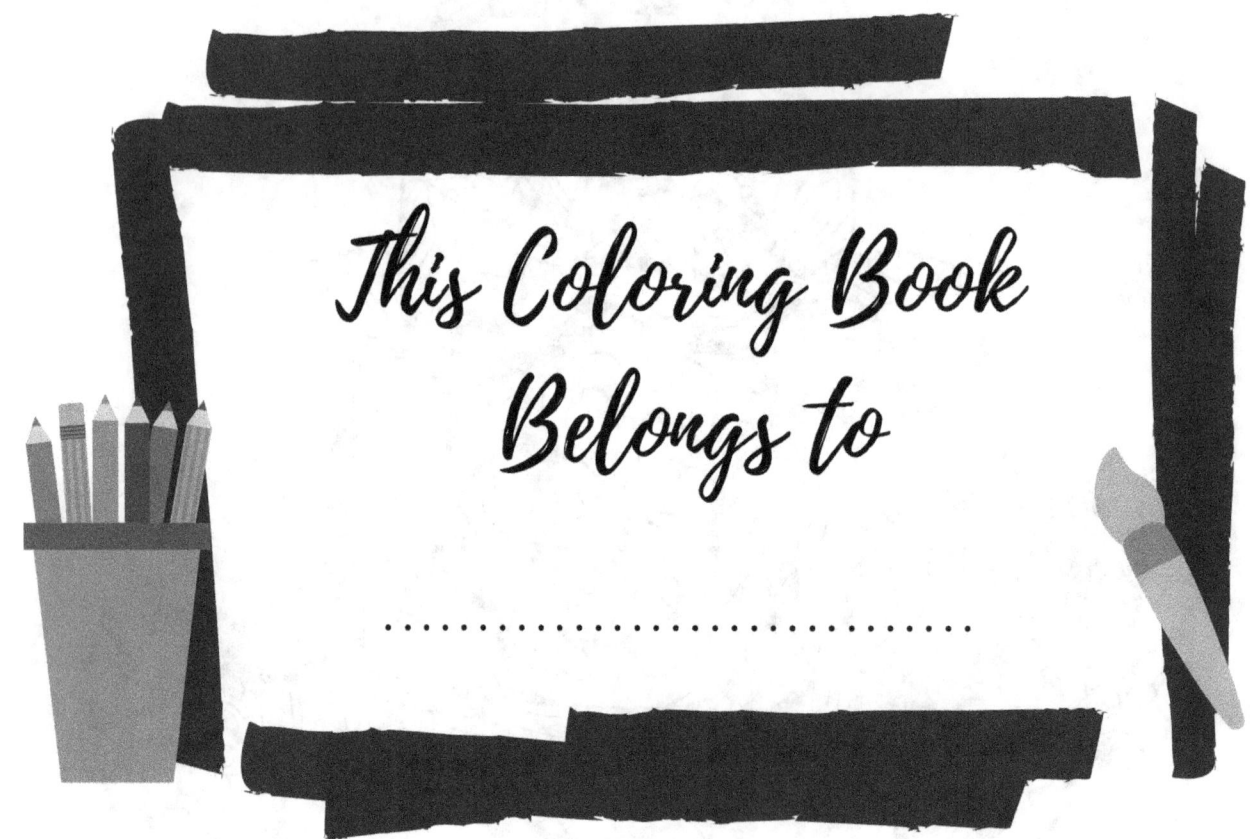

This Coloring Book
Belongs to

....

Special Request

If you liked this book, would you please leave a kind review, it only takes few minutes but will definitely make my day... my month... my year!
Thank you in advance.

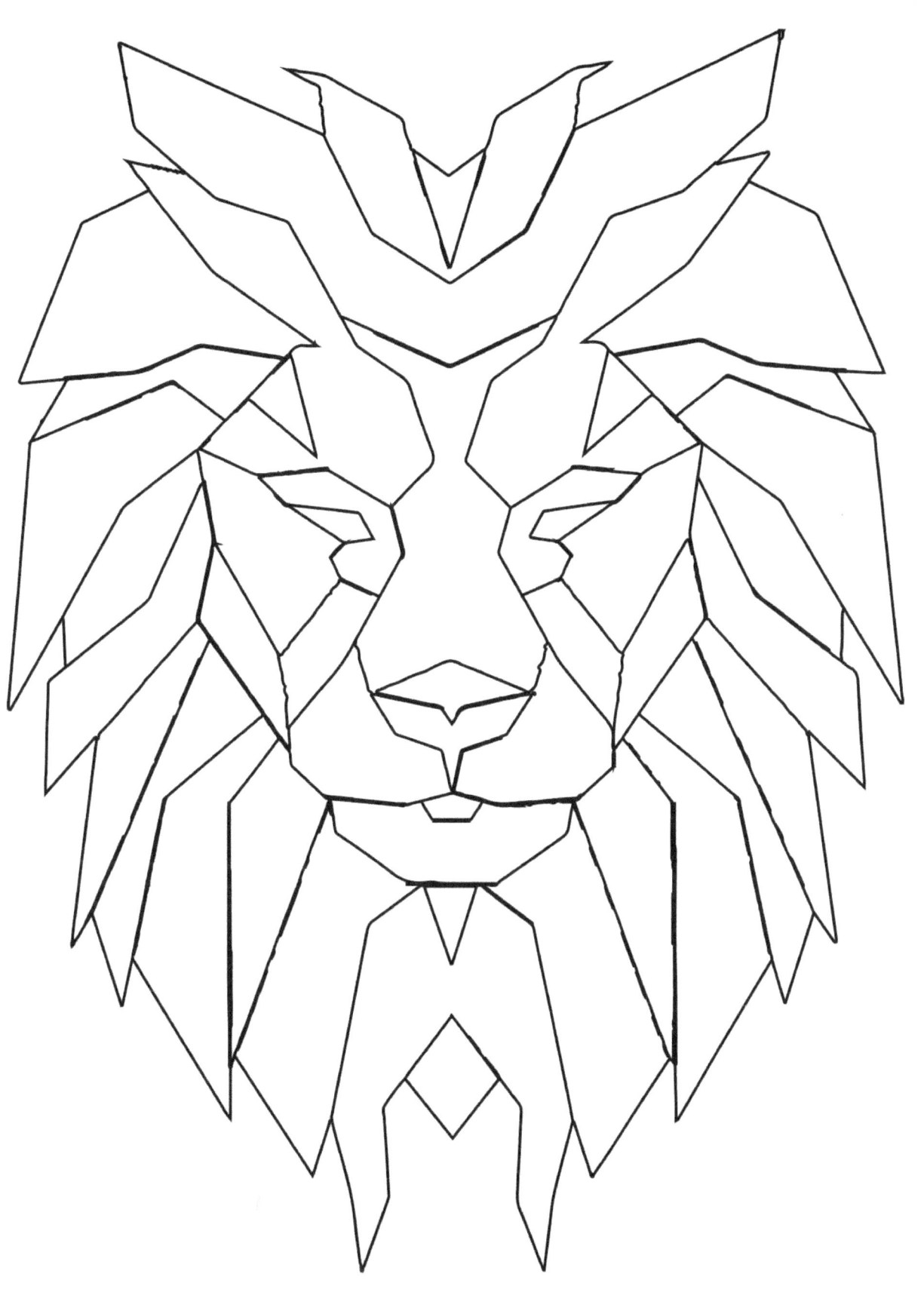

DIFFICULTY LEVEL: EASY

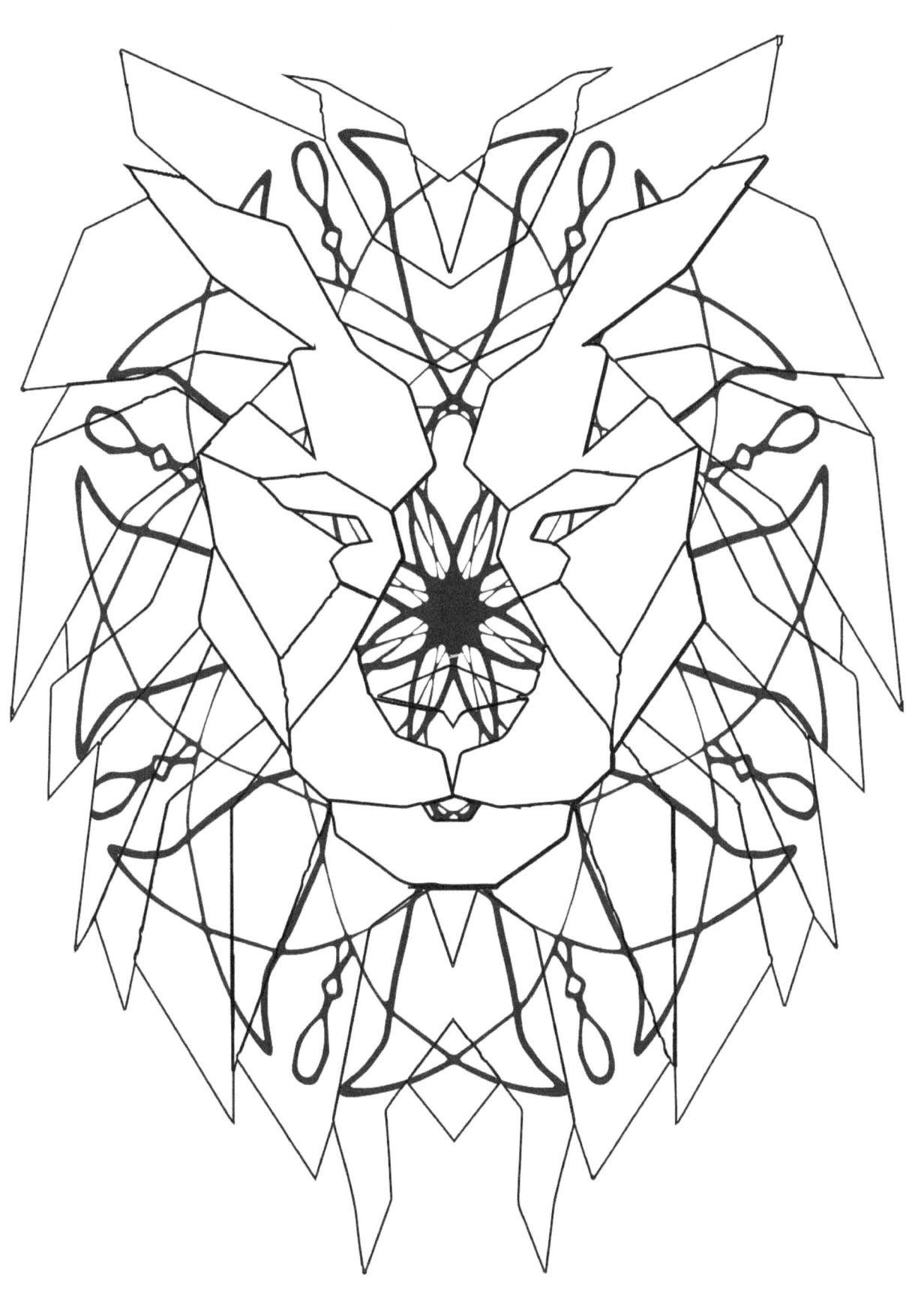

DIFFICULTY LEVEL: INTERMEDIATE

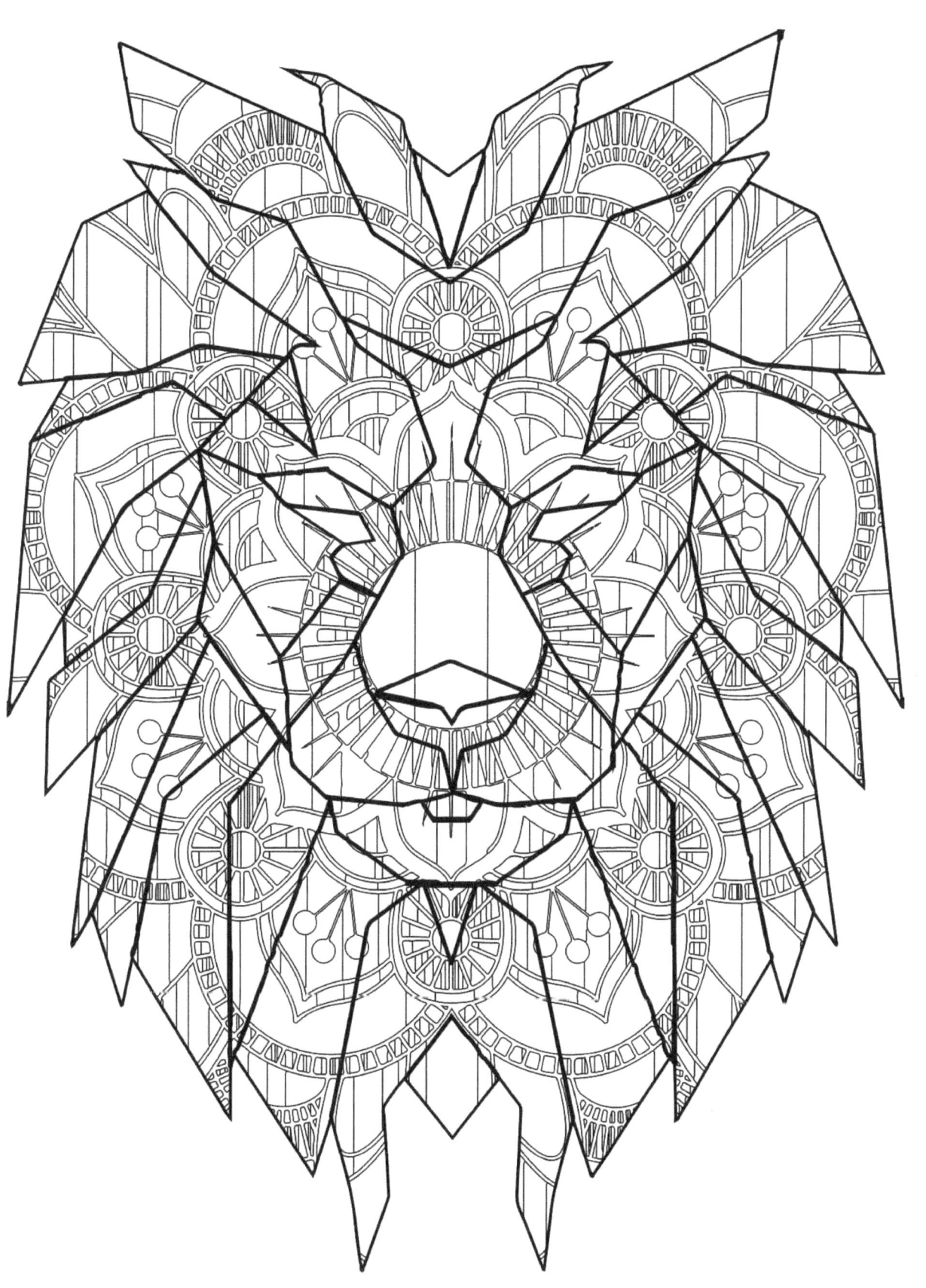

DIFFICULTY LEVEL: CHALLENGING

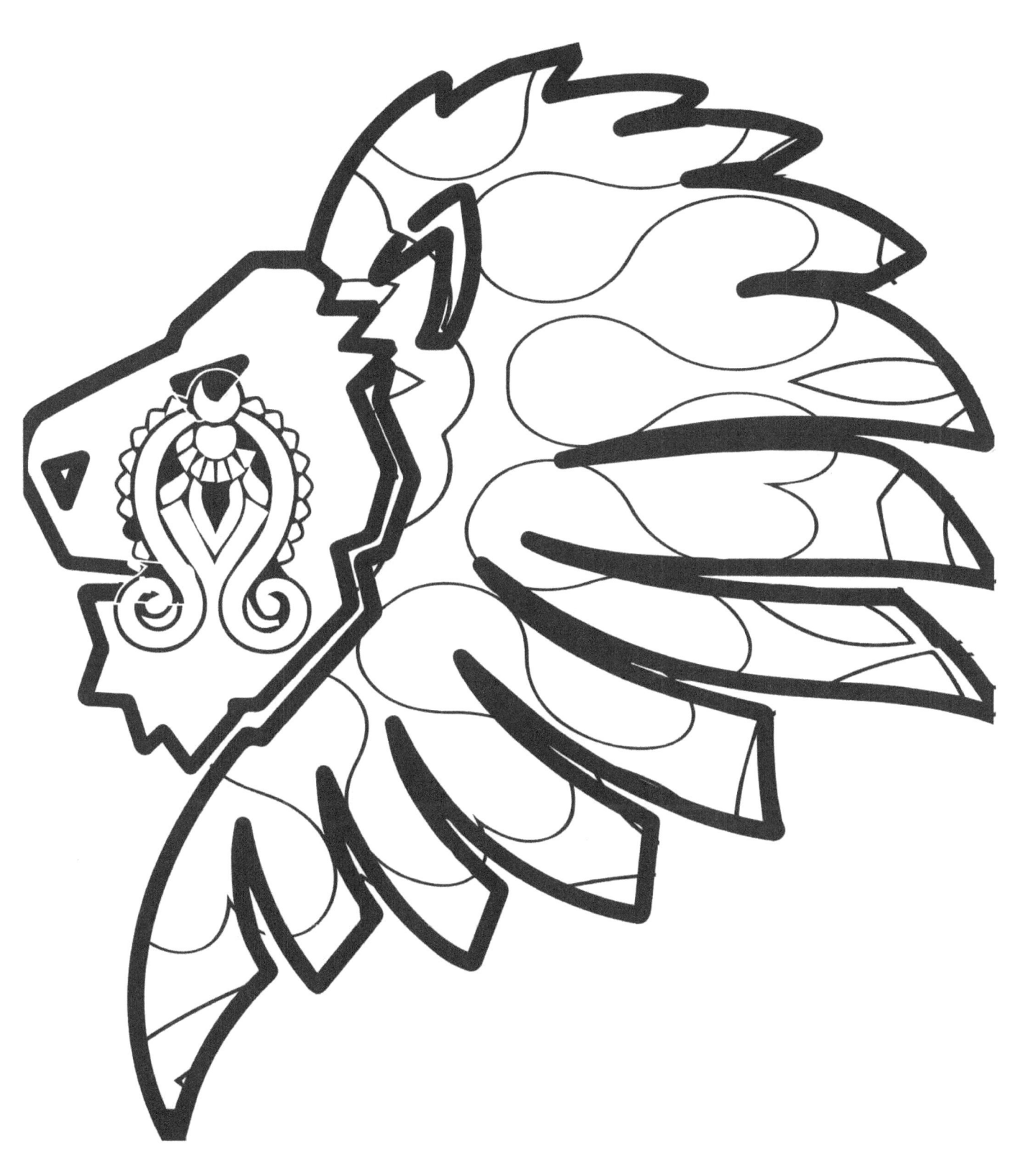

DIFFICULTY LEVEL: EASY

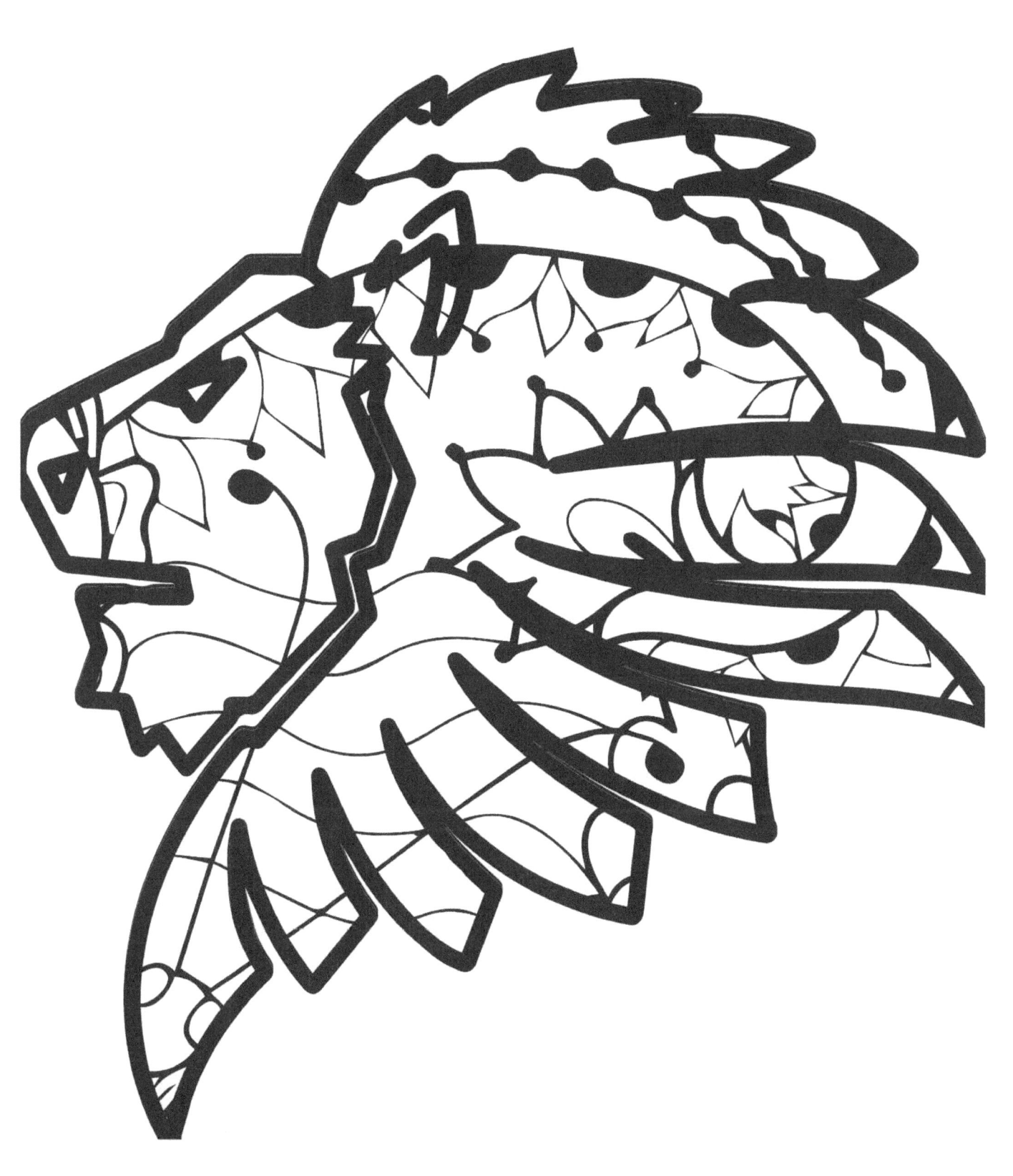

DIFFICULTY LEVEL: INTERMEDIATE

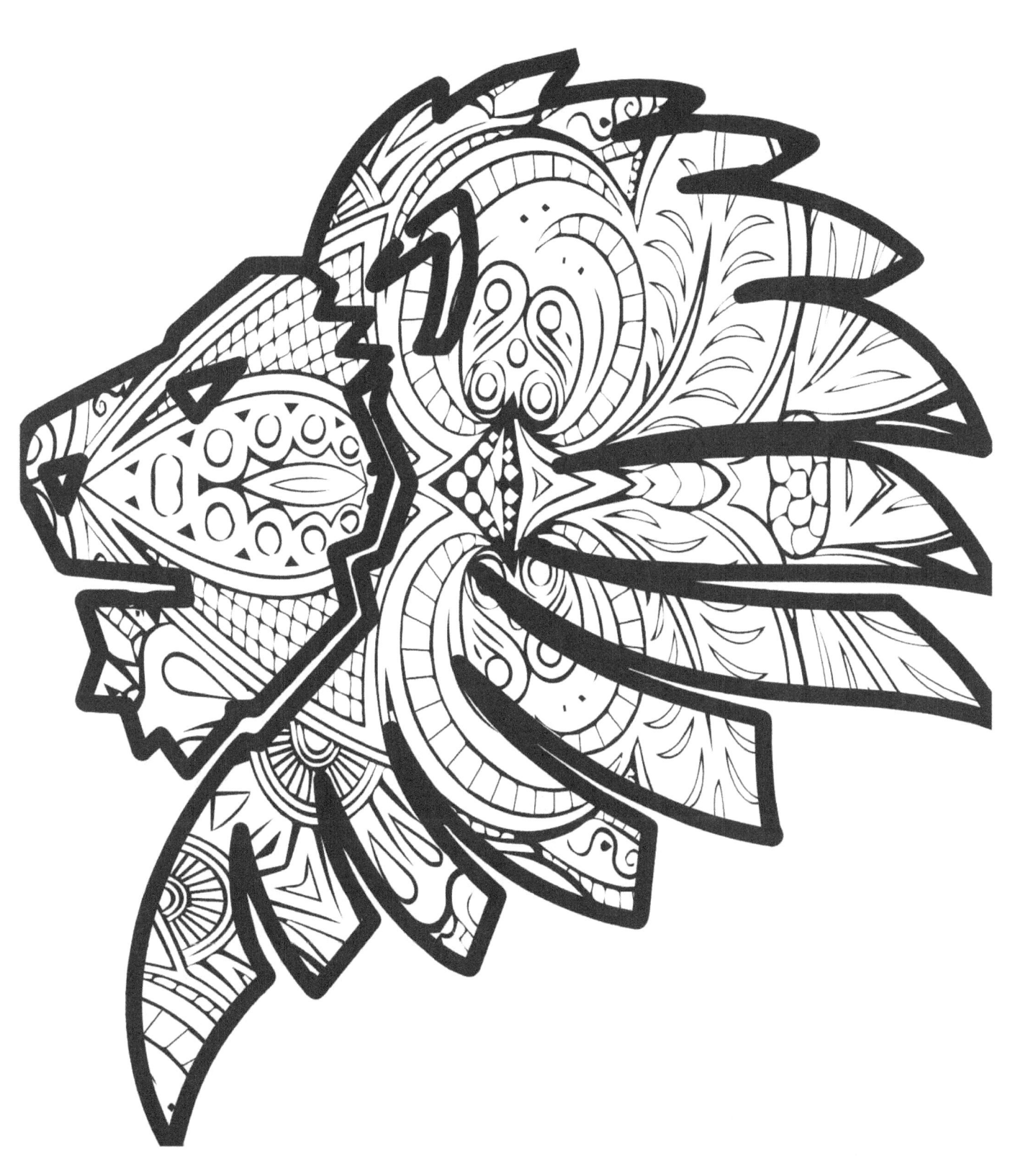

DIFFICULTY LEVEL: CHALLENGING

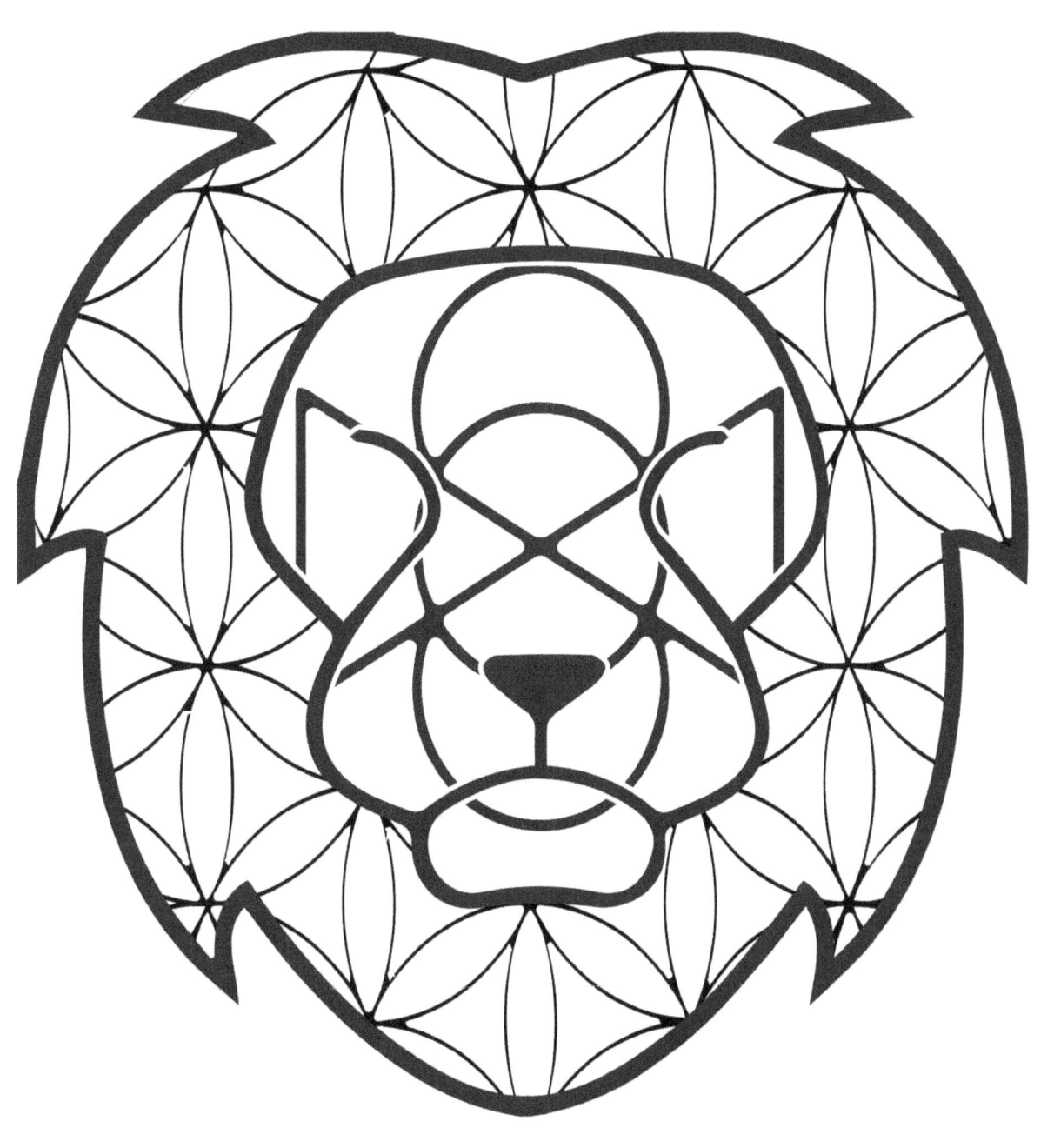

DIFFICULTY LEVEL: EASY

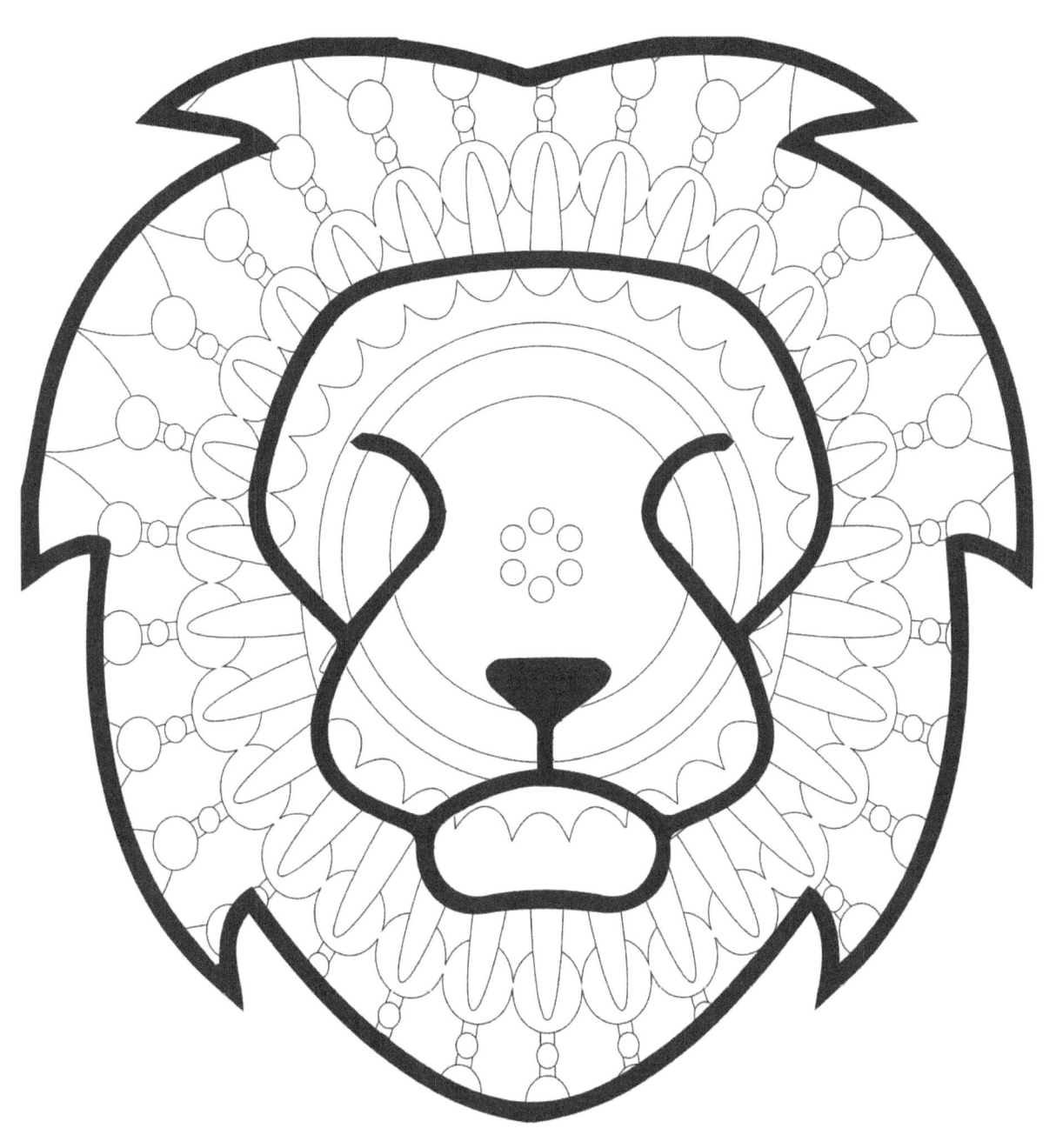

DIFFICULTY LEVEL: INTERMEDIATE

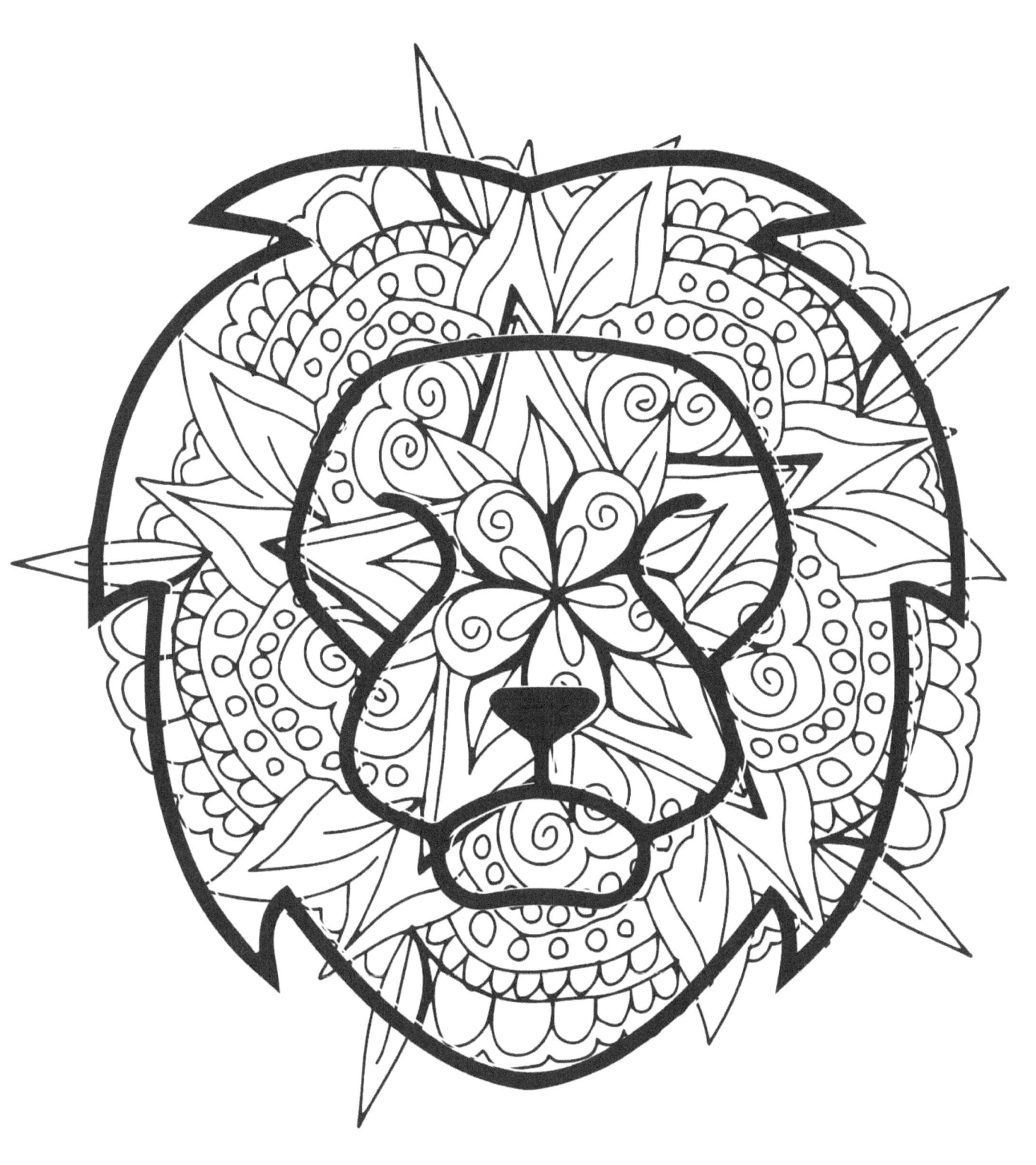

DIFFICULTY LEVEL: CHALLENGING

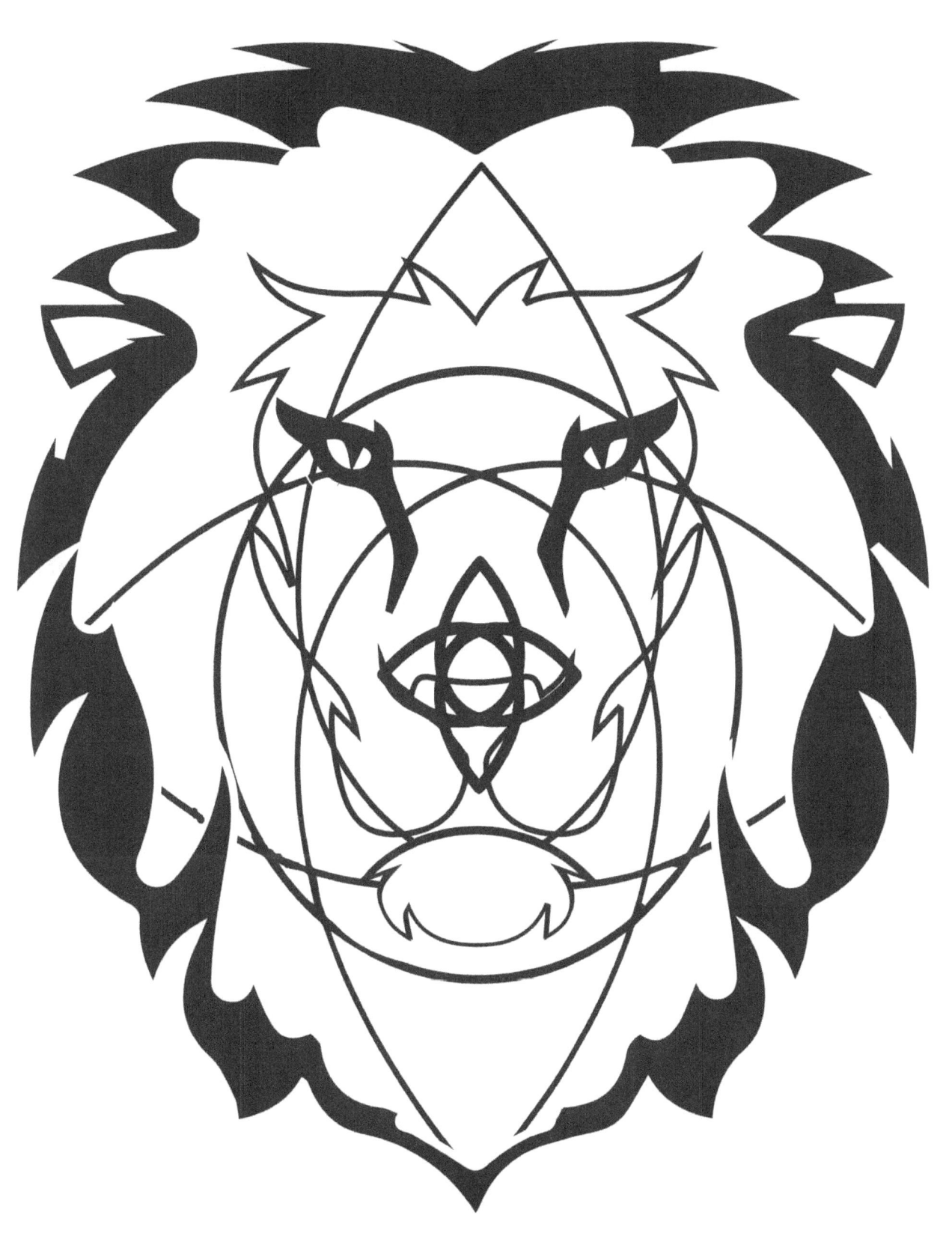

DIFFICULTY LEVEL: EASY

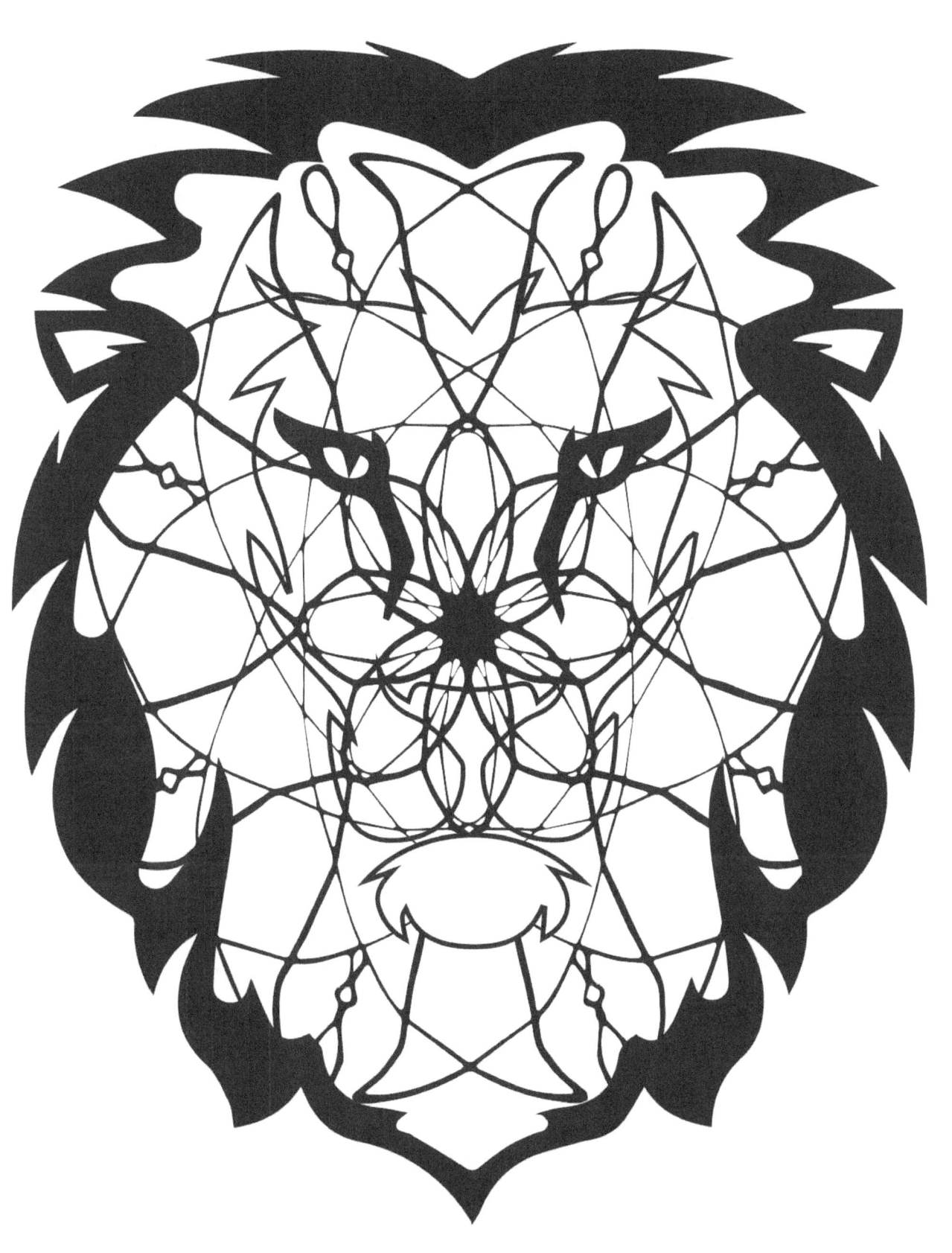

DIFFICULTY LEVEL: INTERMEDIATE

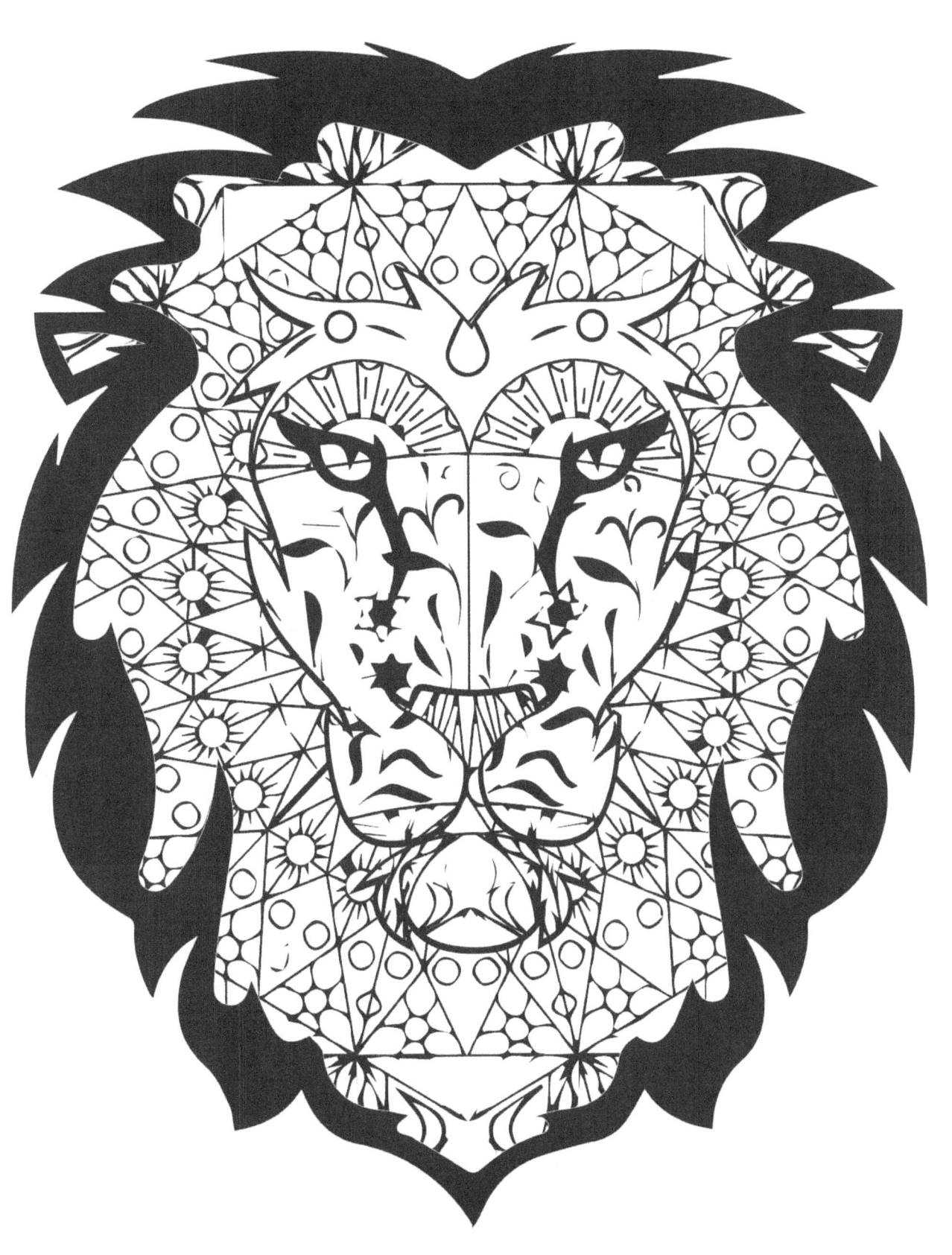

DIFFICULTY LEVEL: CHALLENGING

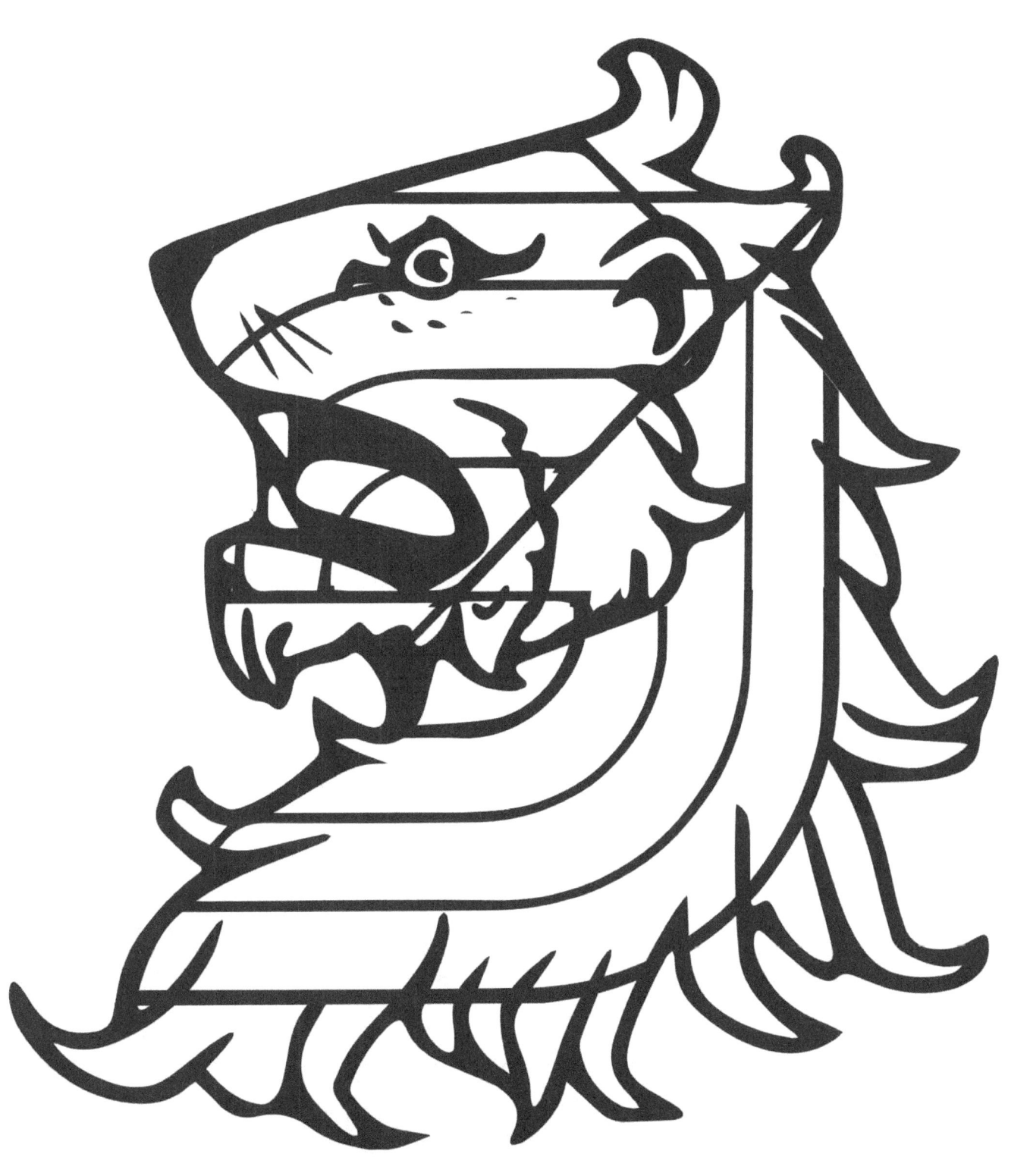

DIFFICULTY LEVEL: EASY

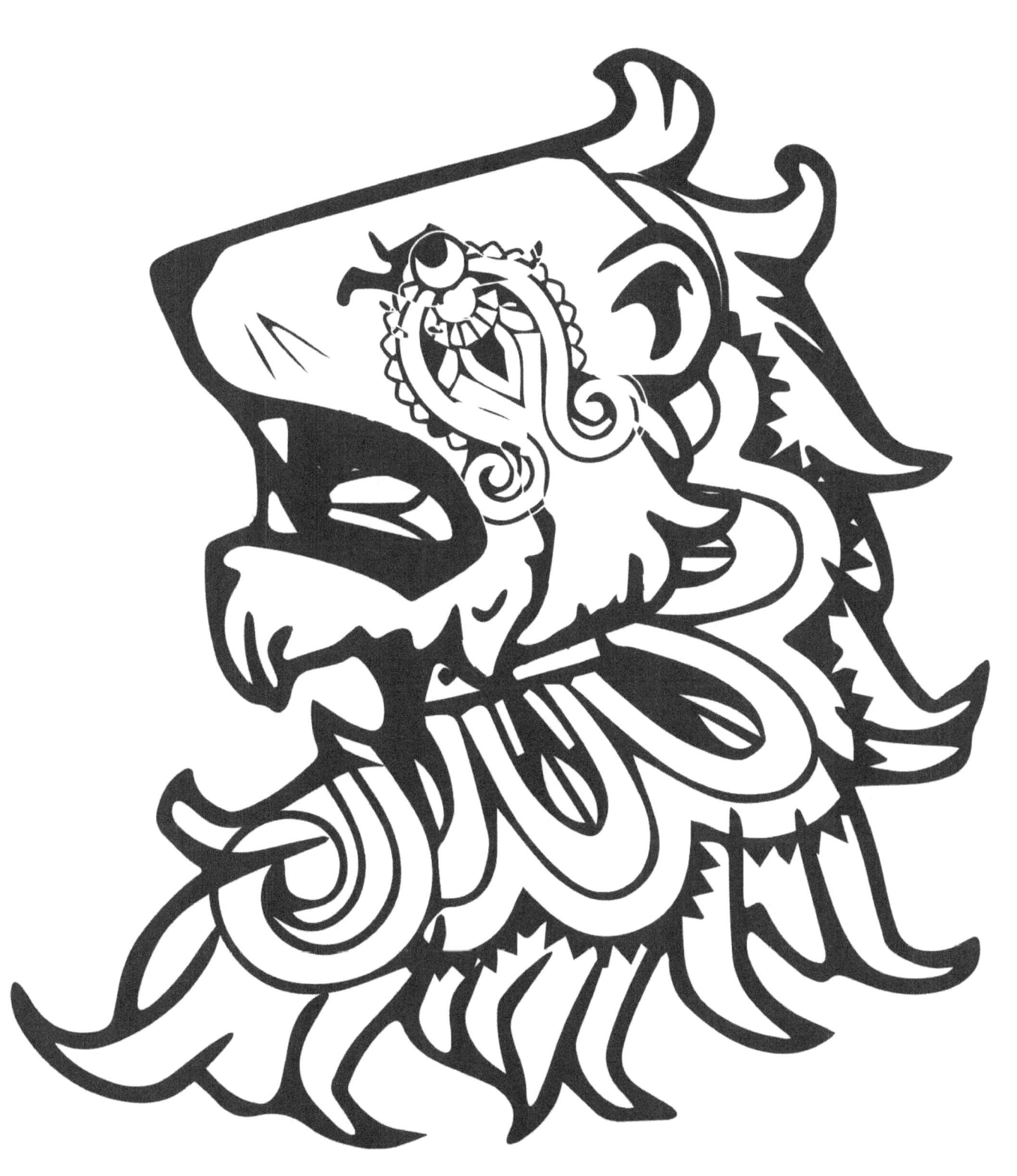

DIFFICULTY LEVEL: INTERMEDIATE

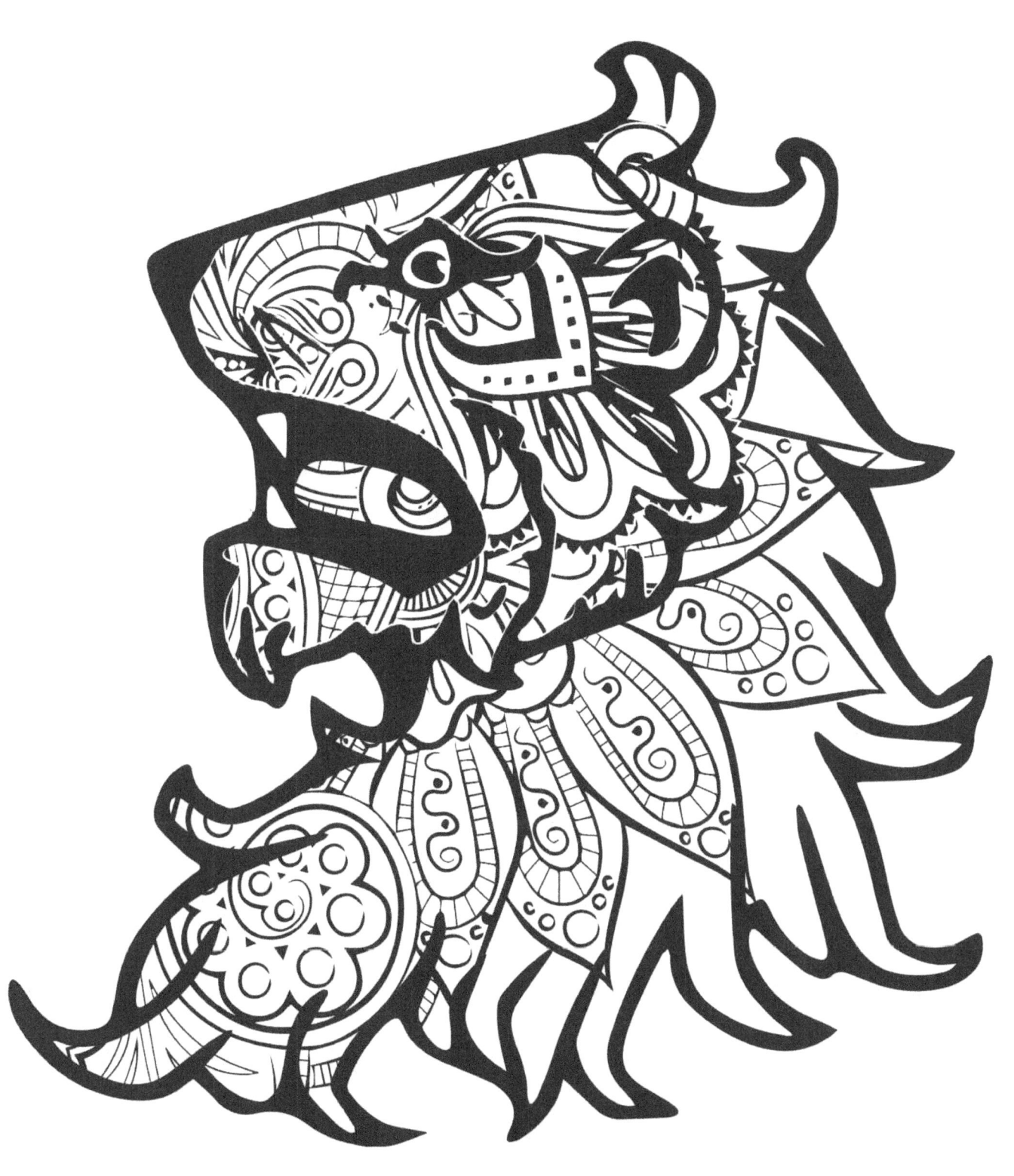

DIFFICULTY LEVEL: CHALLENGING

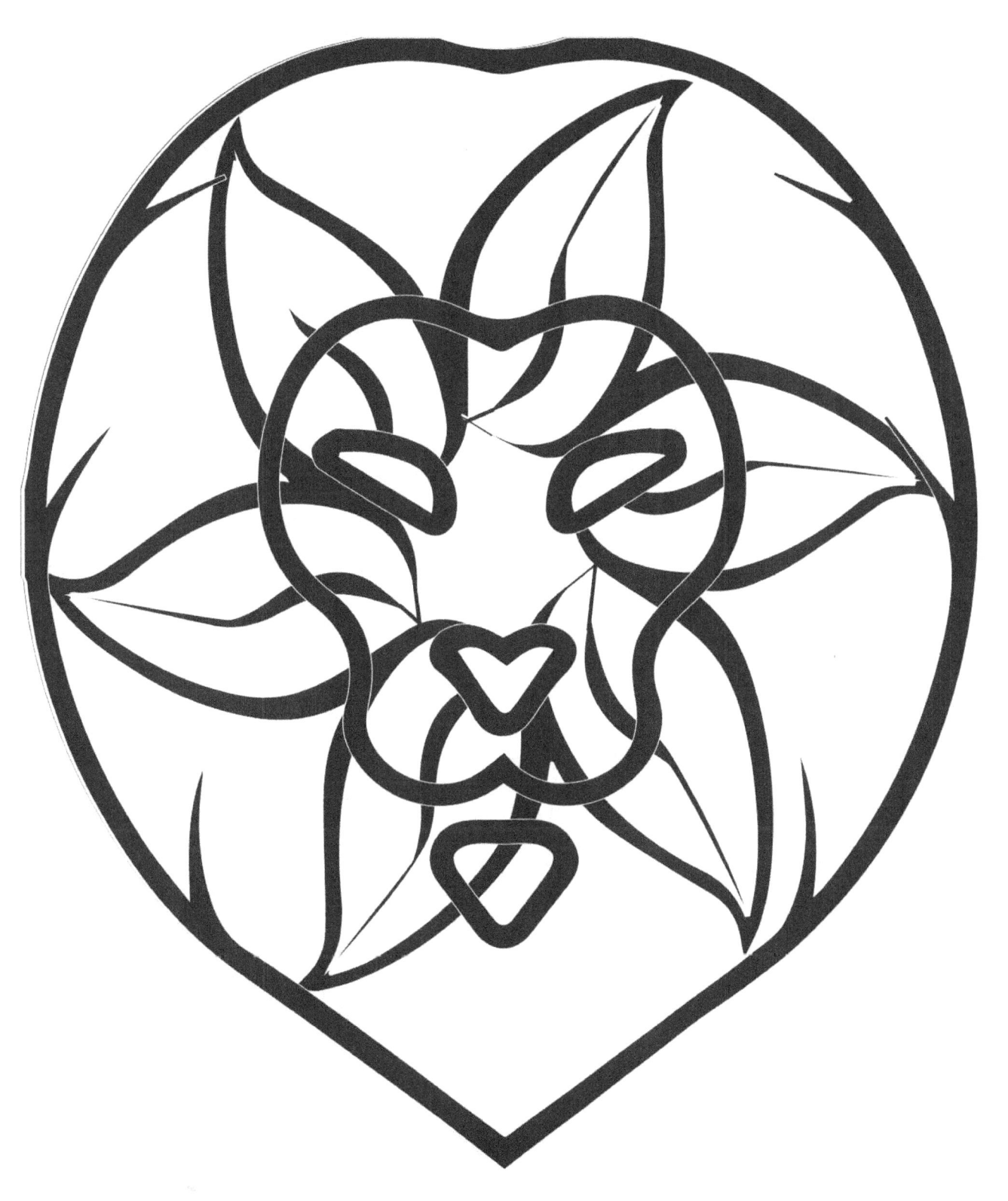

DIFFICULTY LEVEL: EASY

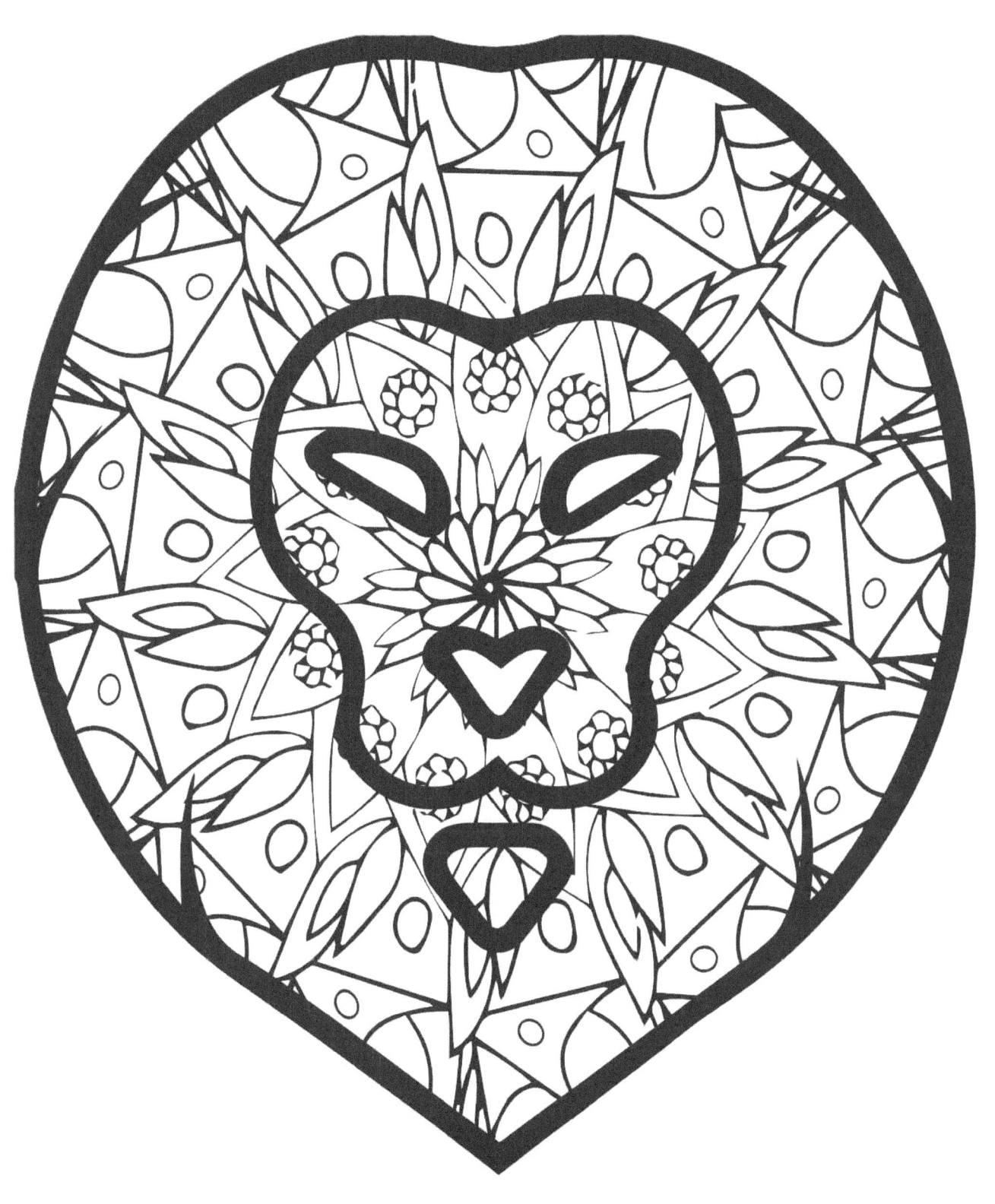

DIFFICULTY LEVEL: INTERMEDIATE

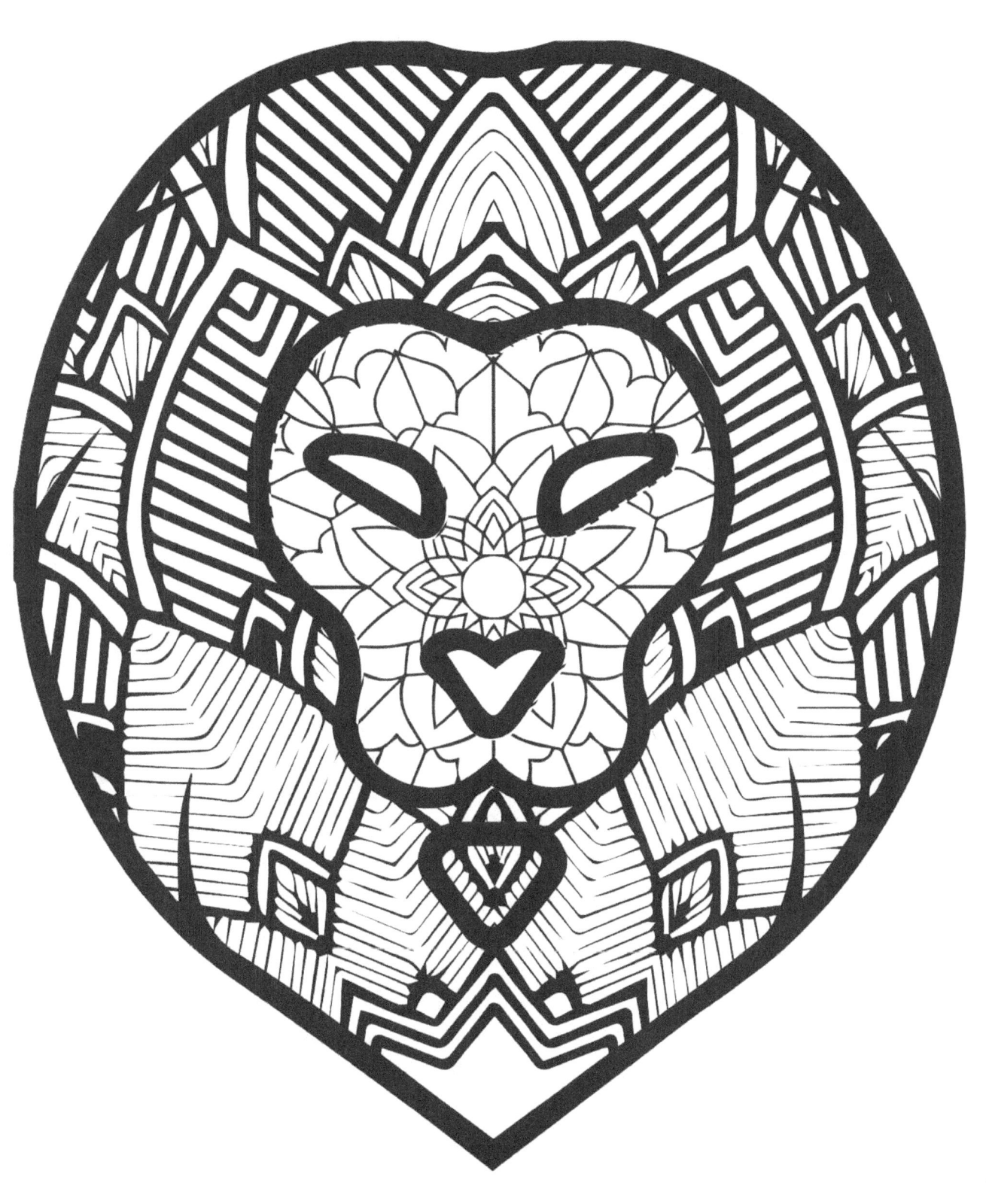

DIFFICULTY LEVEL: CHALLENGING

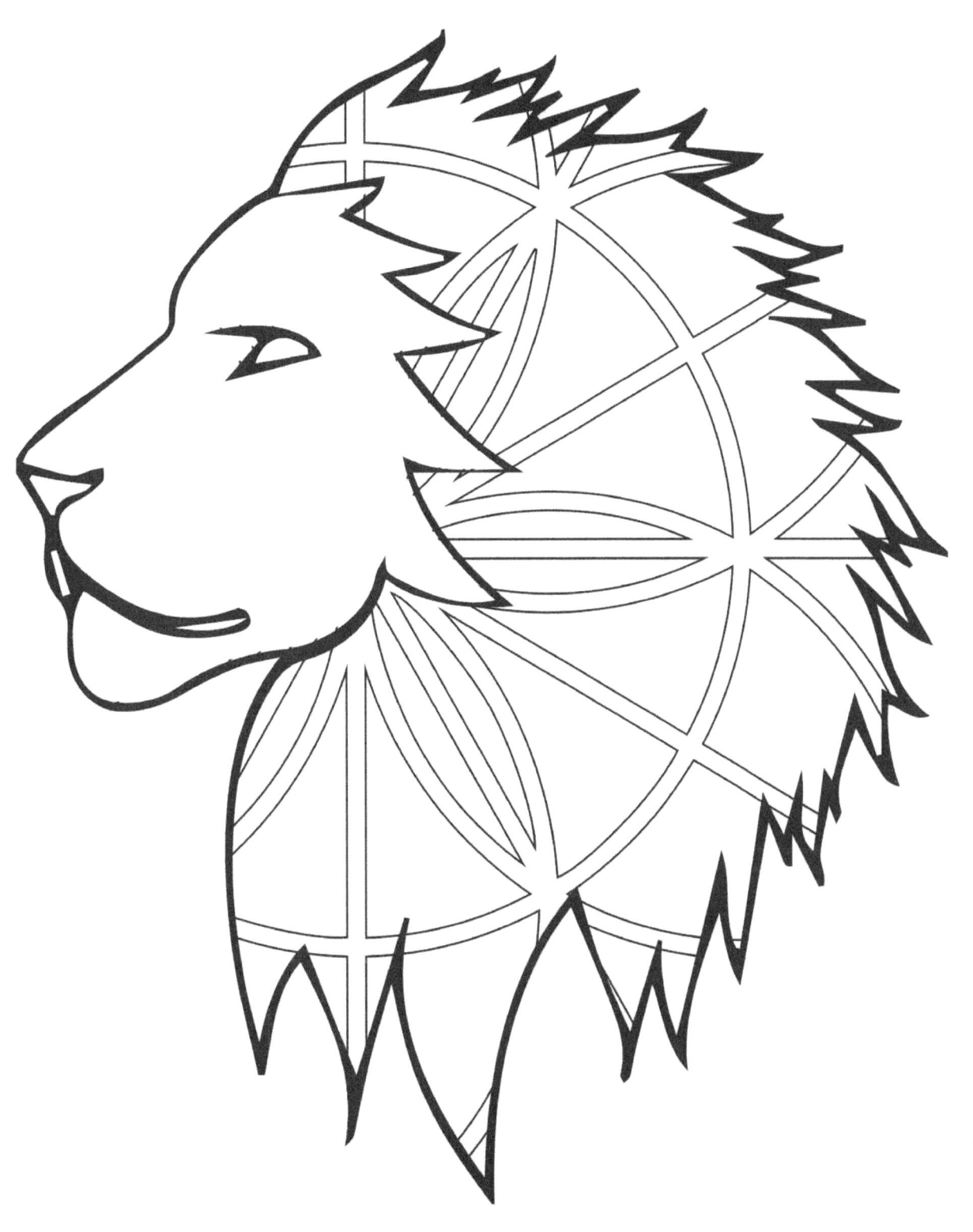

DIFFICULTY LEVEL: EASY

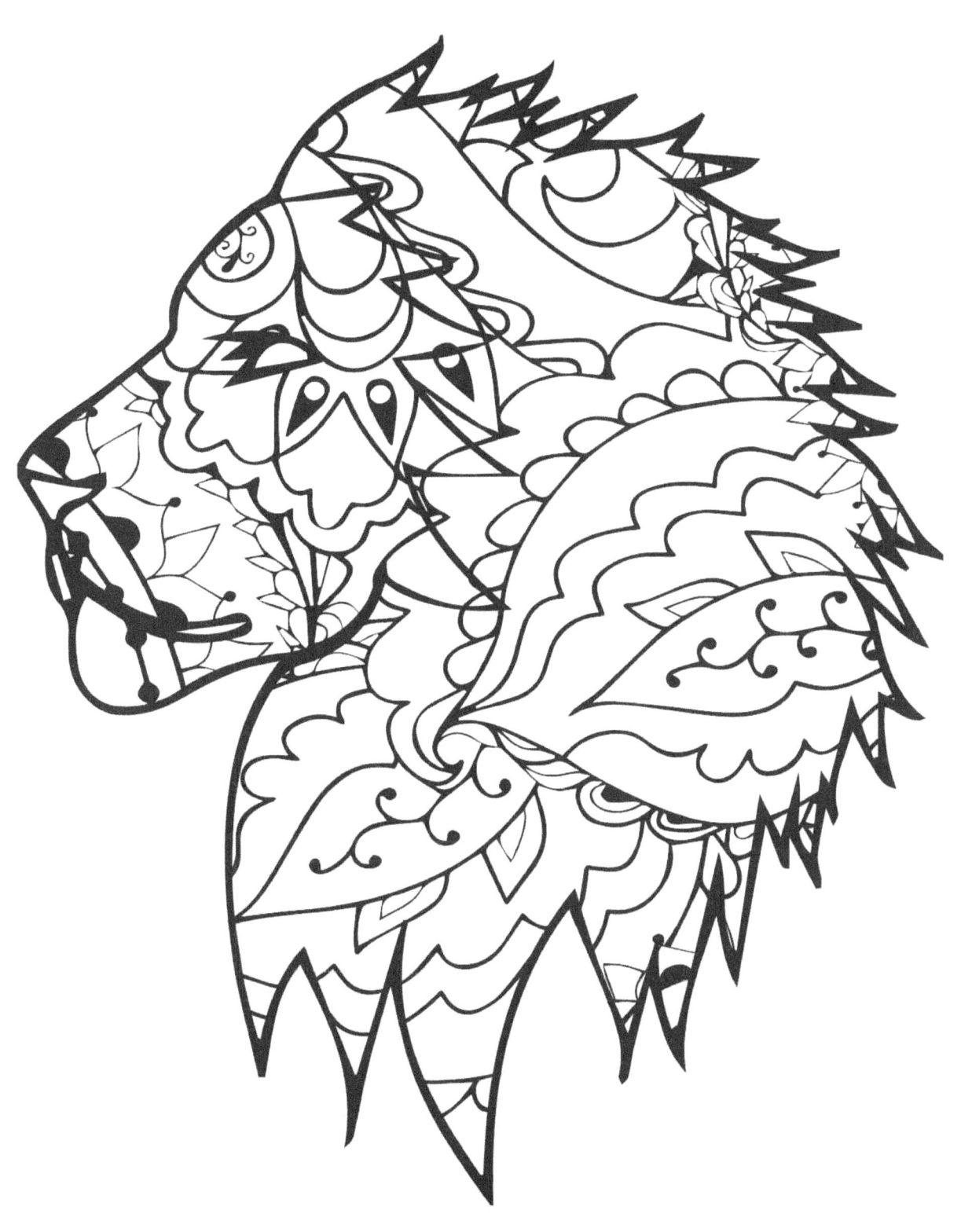

DIFFICULTY LEVEL: INTERMEDIATE

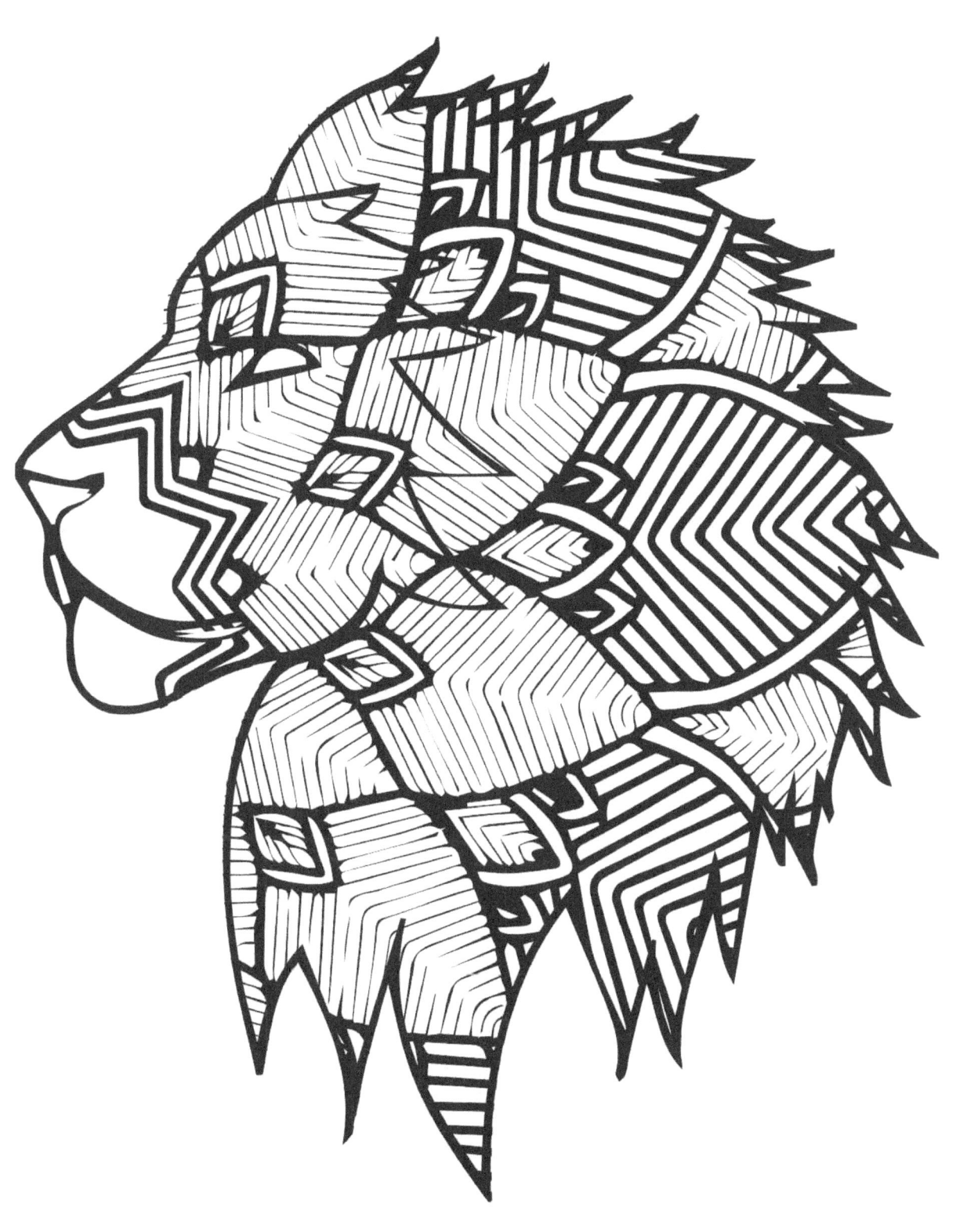

DIFFICULTY LEVEL: CHALLENGING

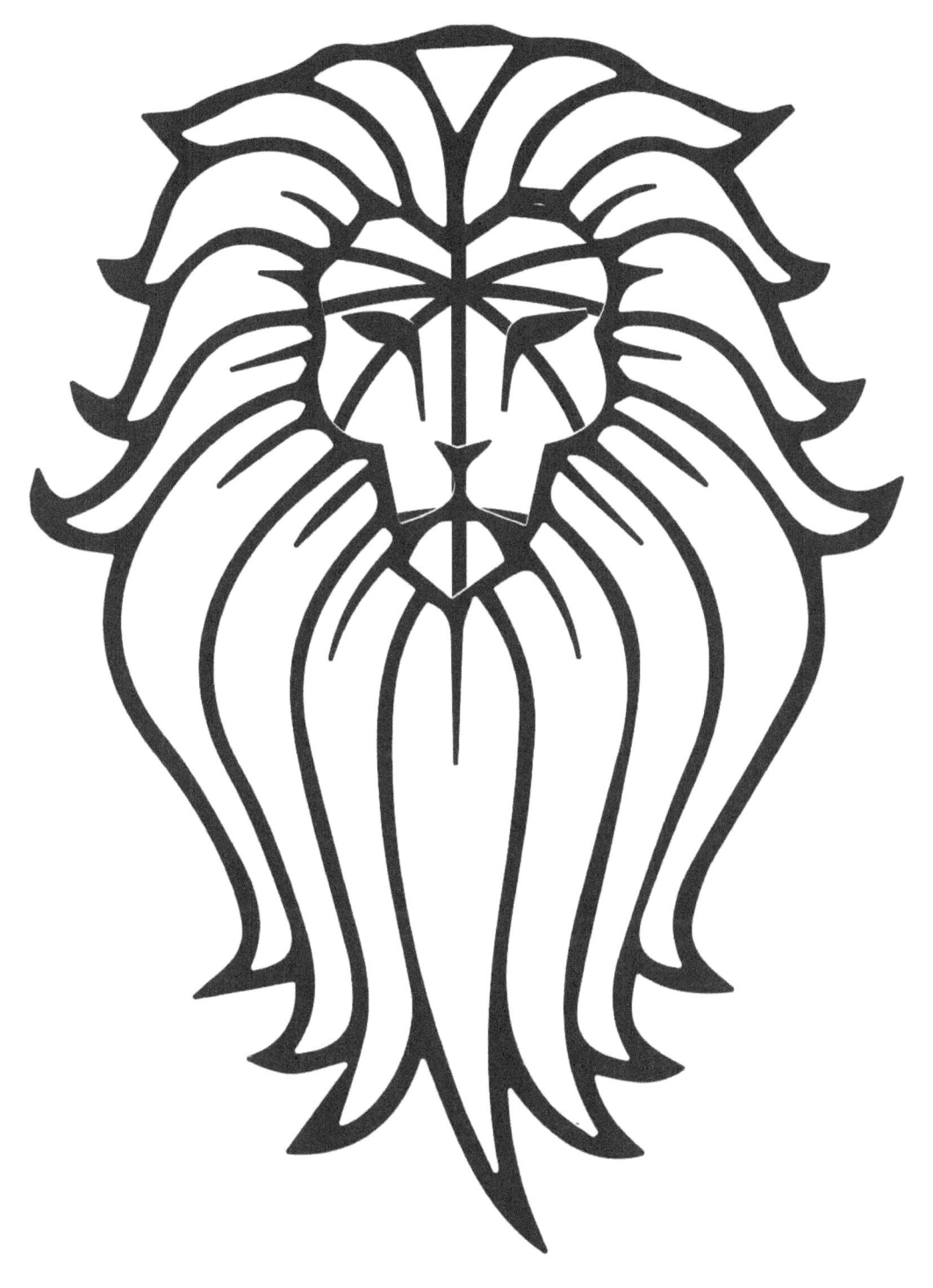

DIFFICULTY LEVEL: EASY

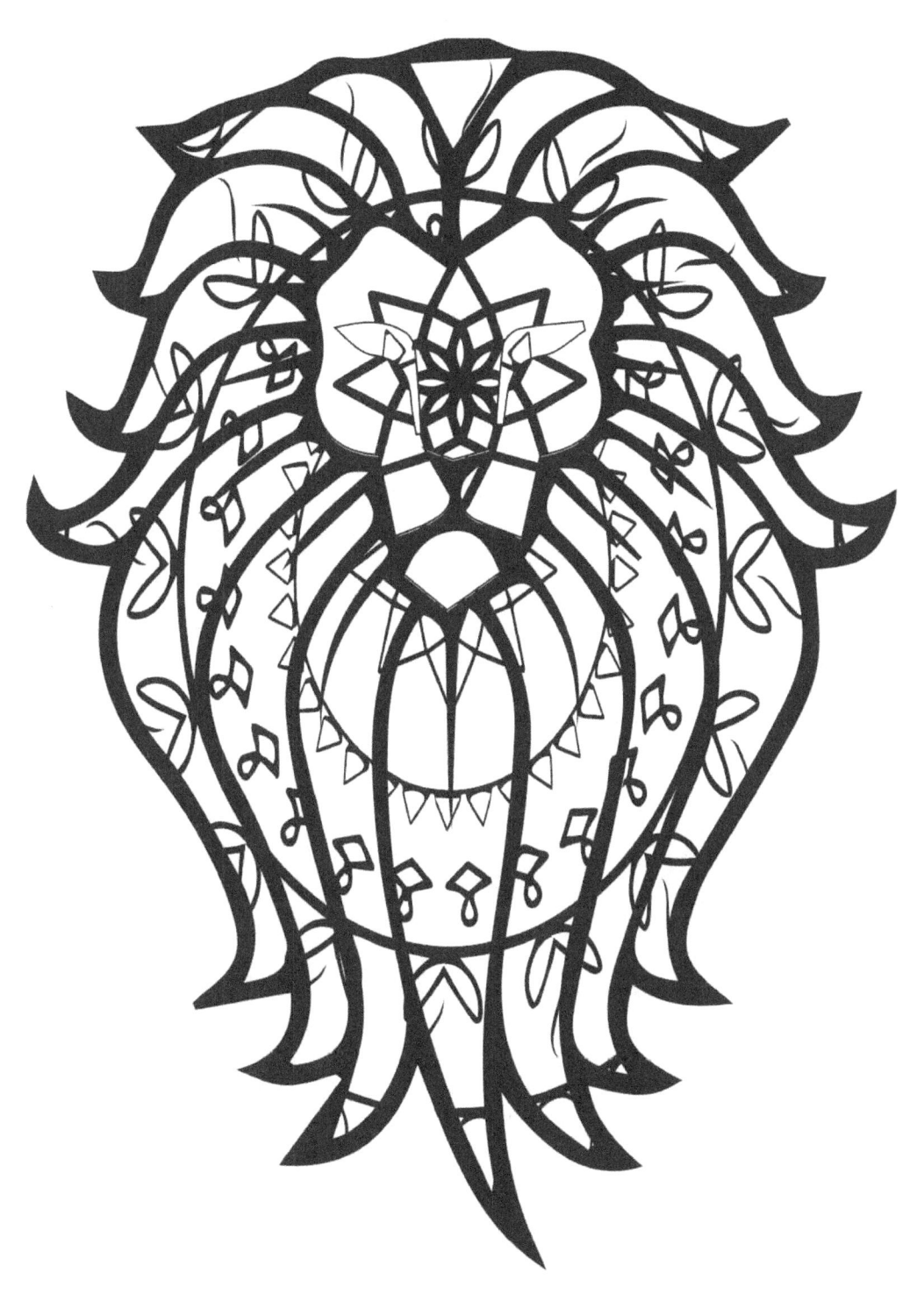

DIFFICULTY LEVEL: INTERMEDIATE

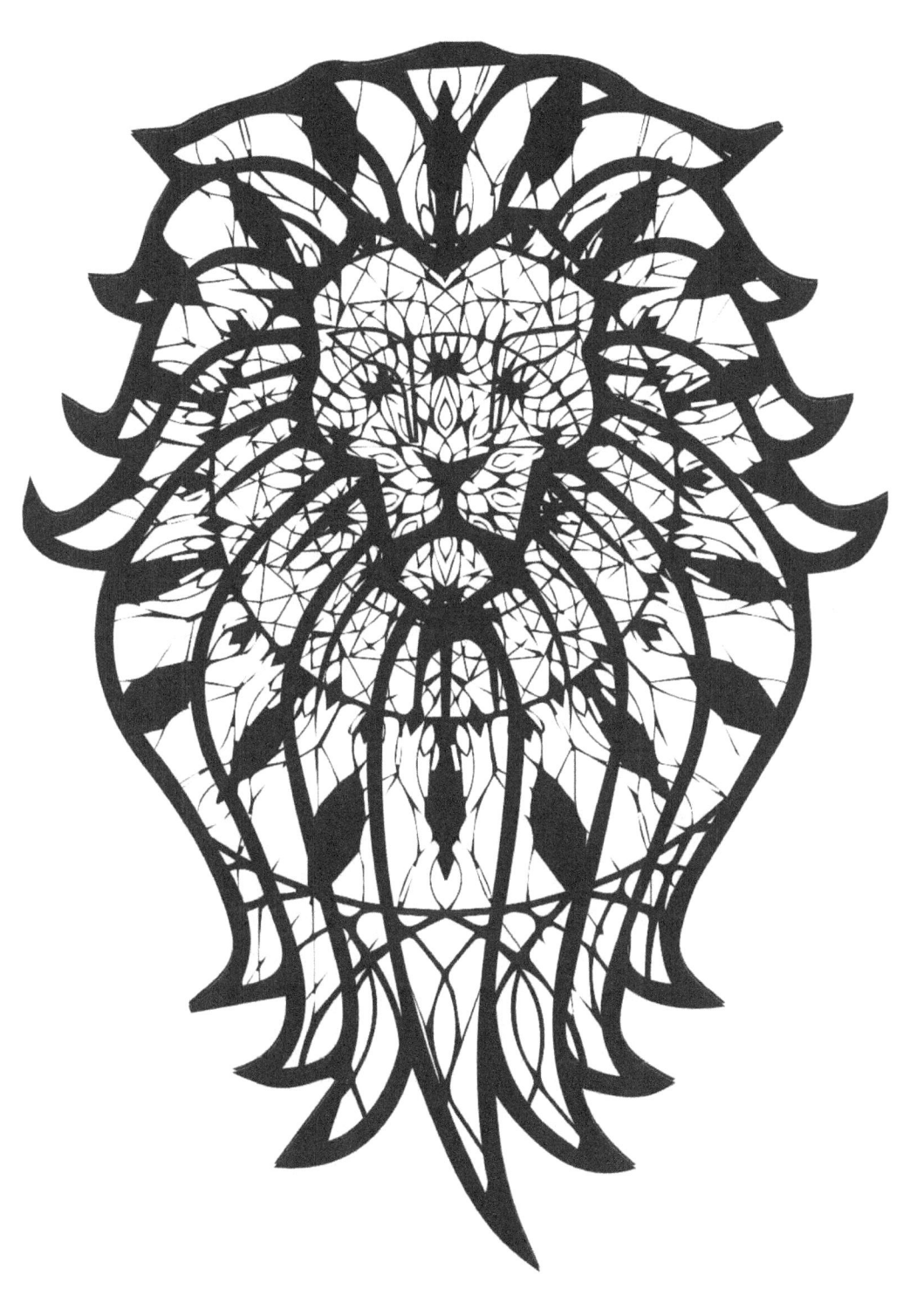

DIFFICULTY LEVEL: CHALLENGING

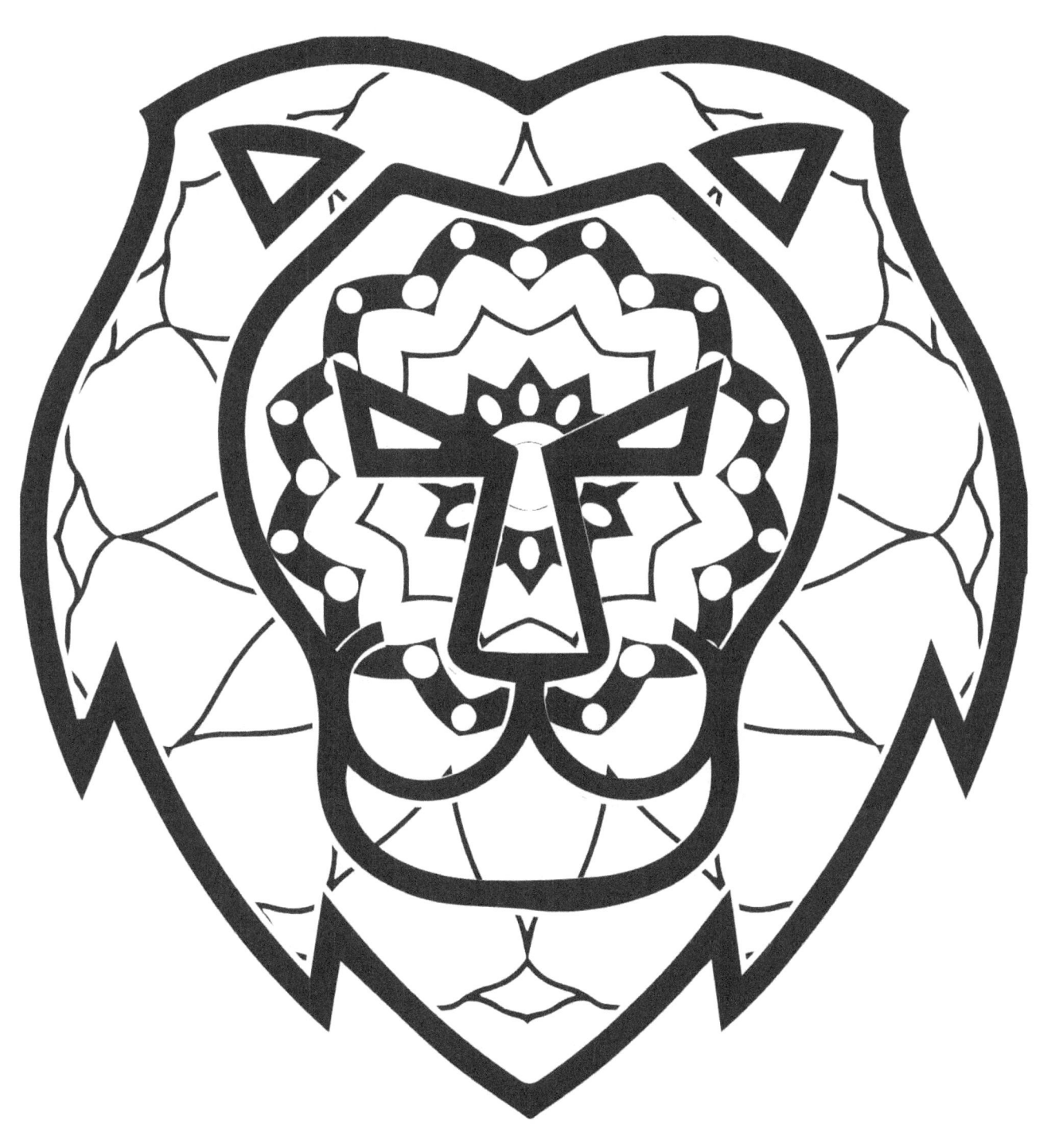

DIFFICULTY LEVEL: EASY

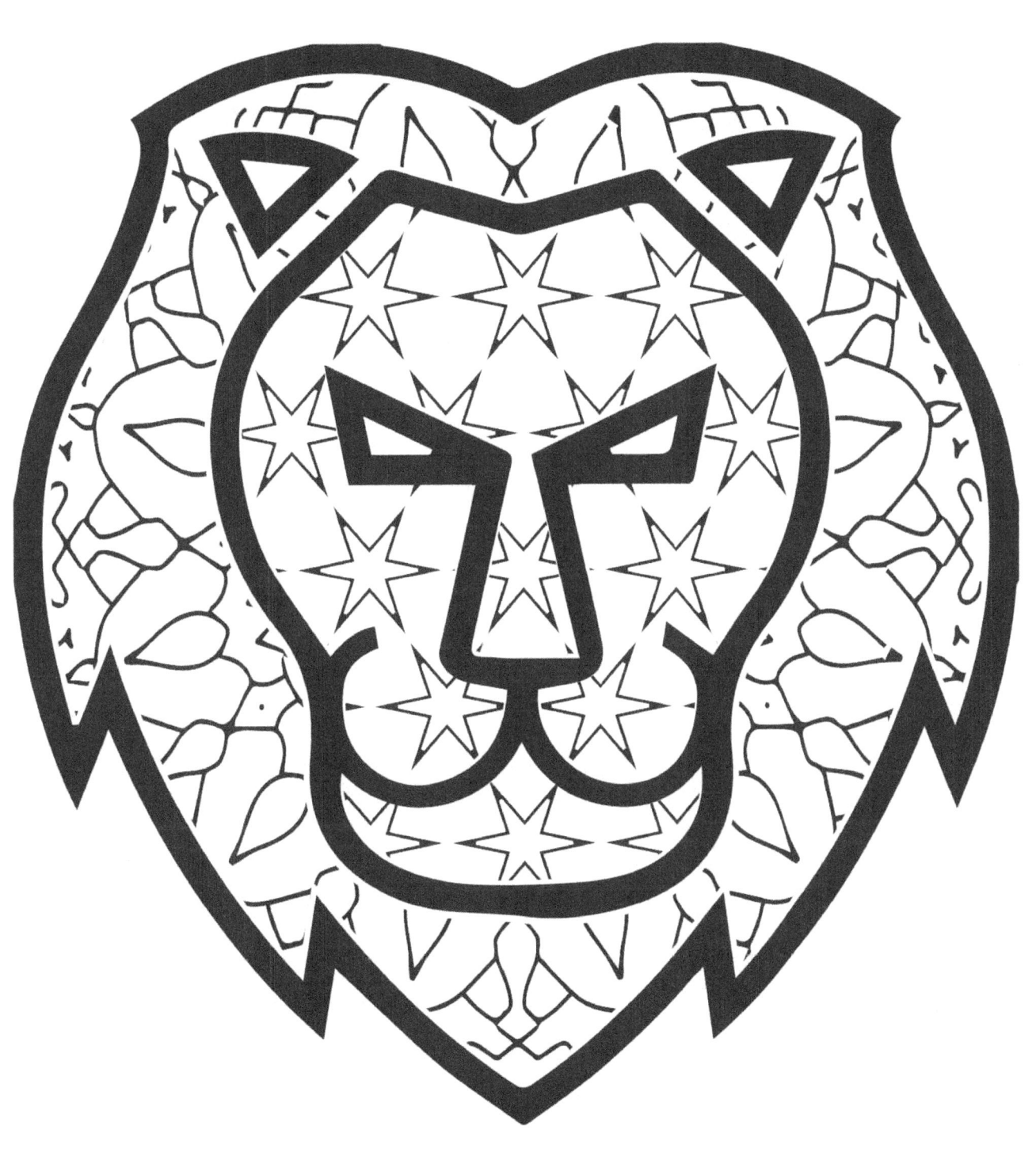

DIFFICULTY LEVEL: INTERMEDIATE

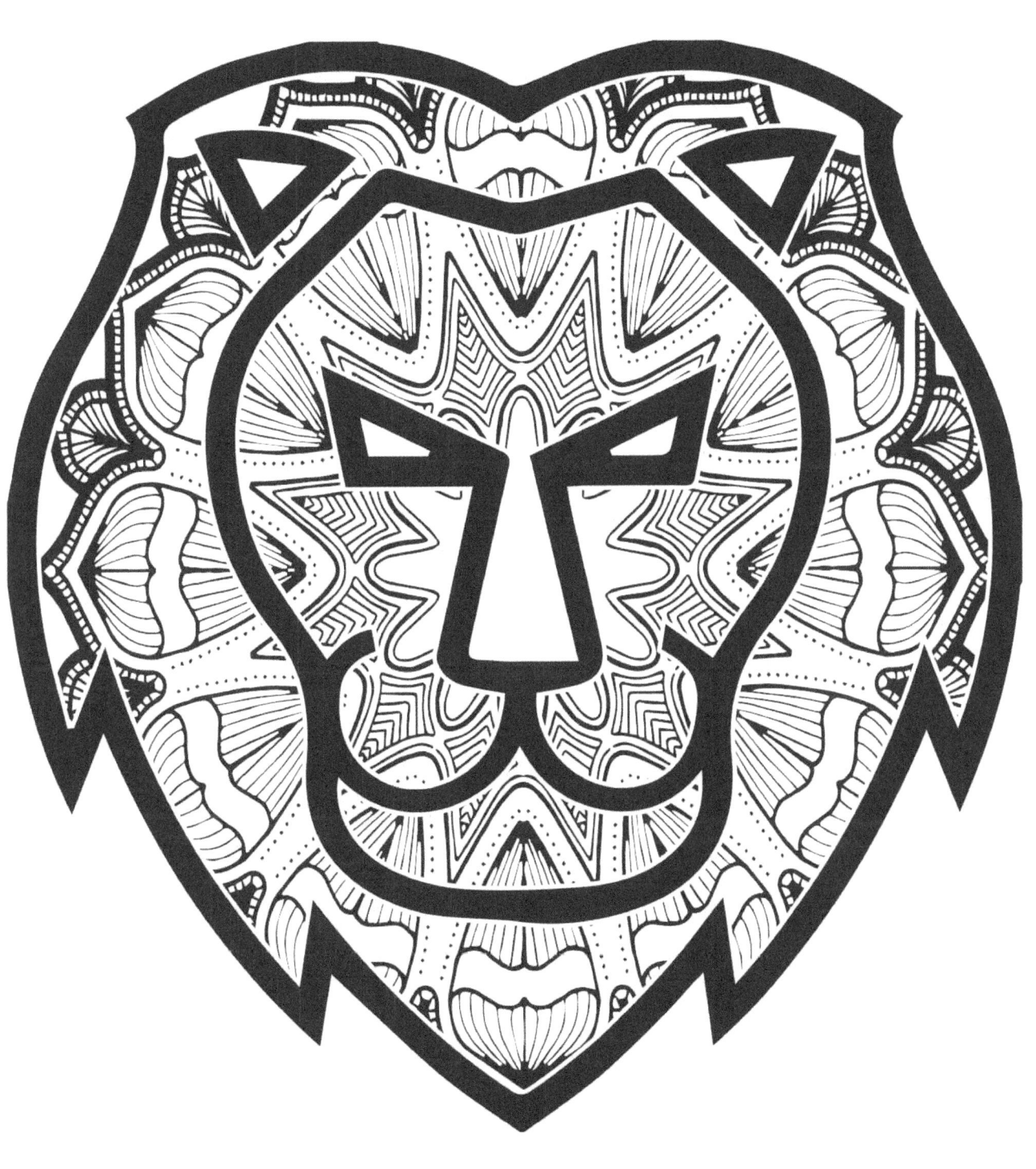

DIFFICULTY LEVEL: CHALLENGING

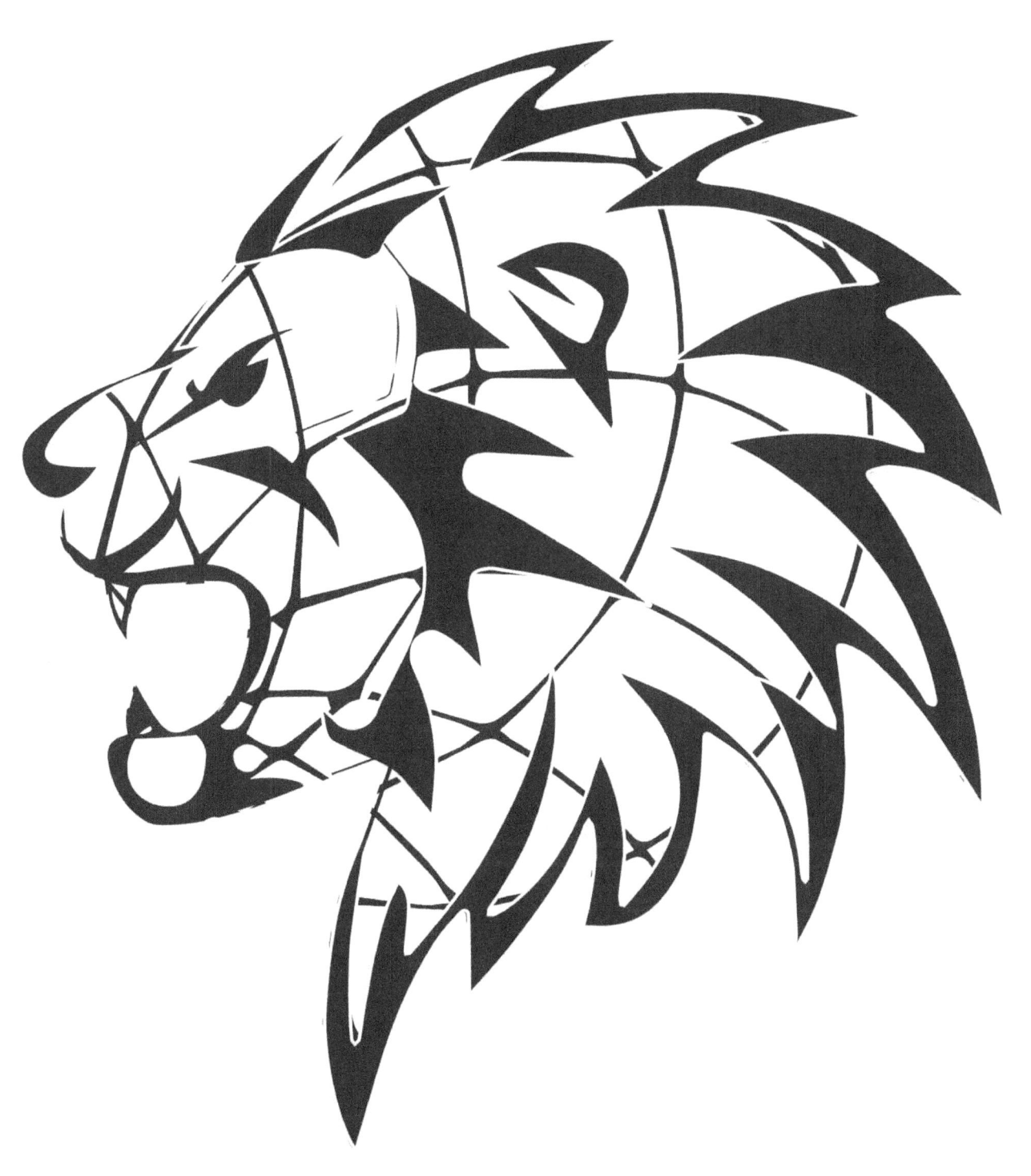

DIFFICULTY LEVEL: EASY

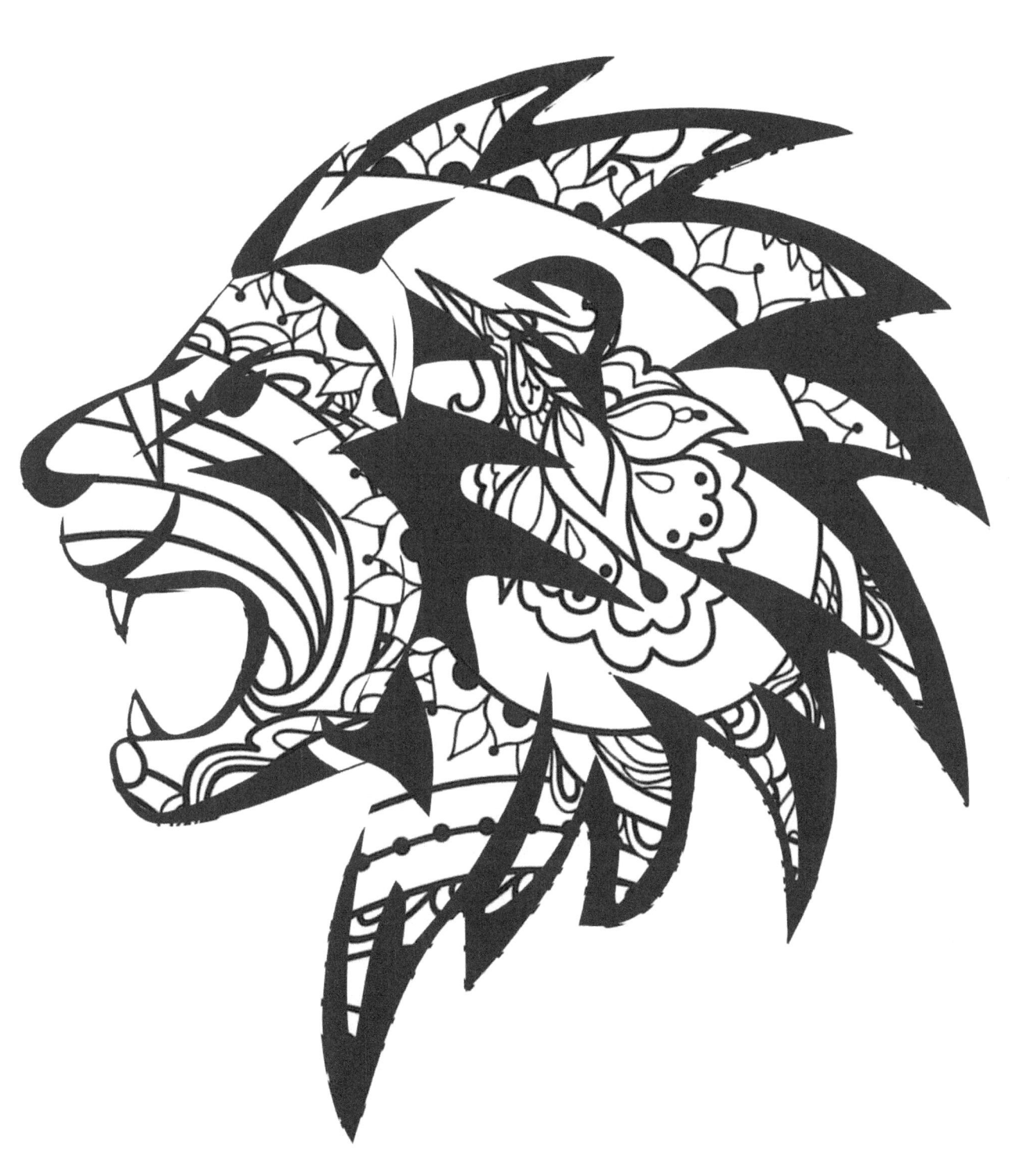

DIFFICULTY LEVEL: INTERMEDIATE

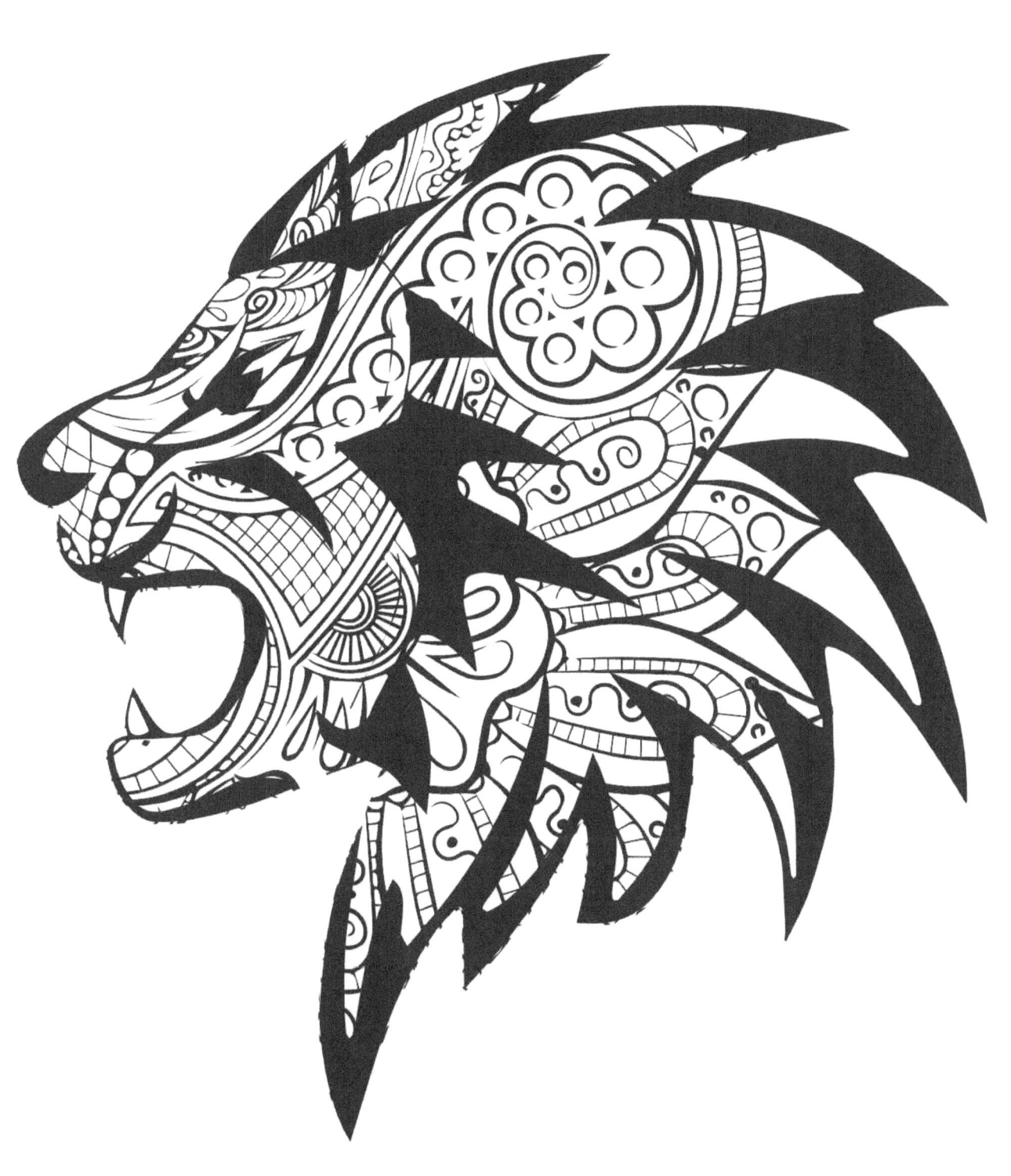

DIFFICULTY LEVEL: CHALLENGING

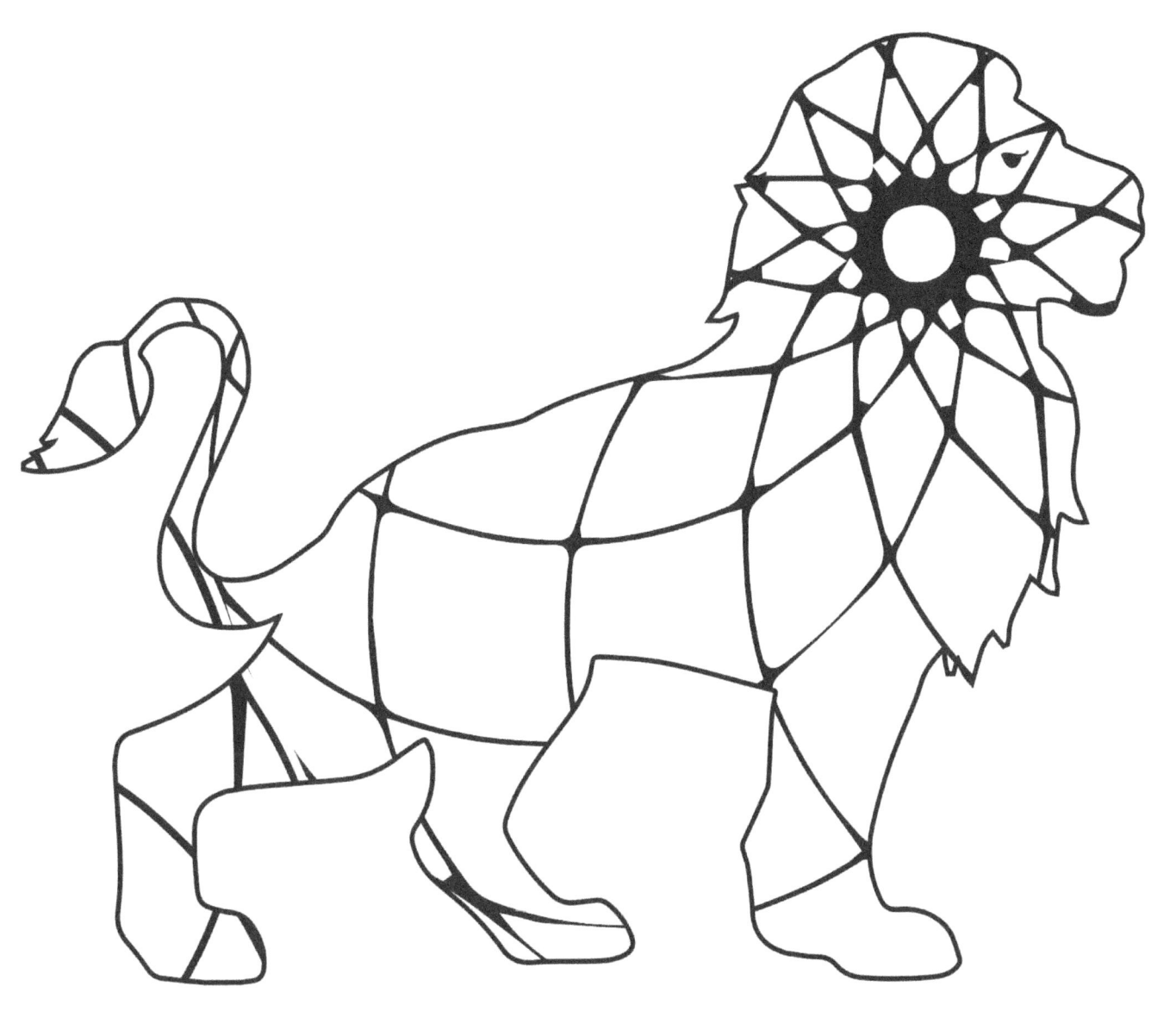

DIFFICULTY LEVEL: EASY

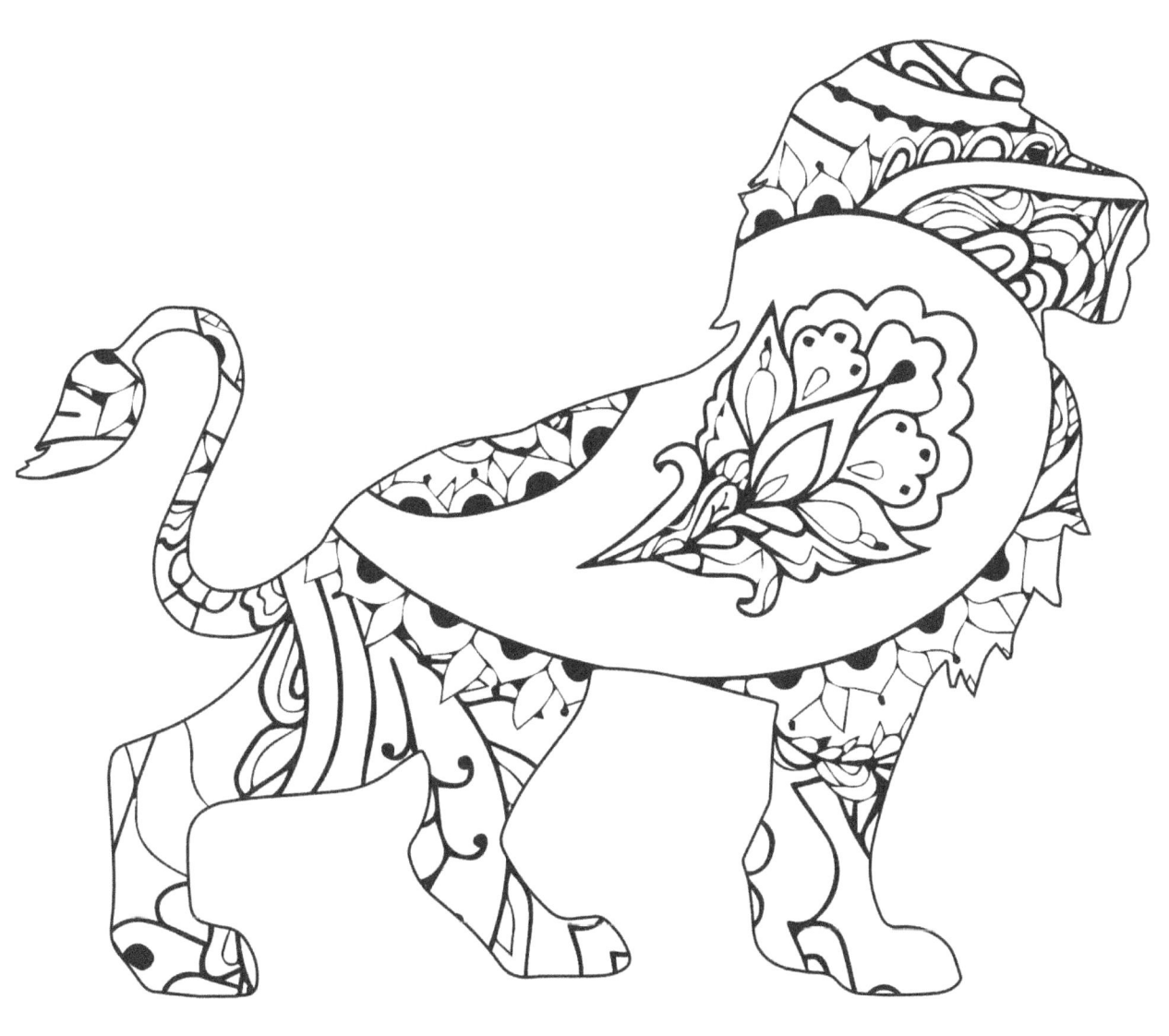

DIFFICULTY LEVEL: INTERMEDIATE

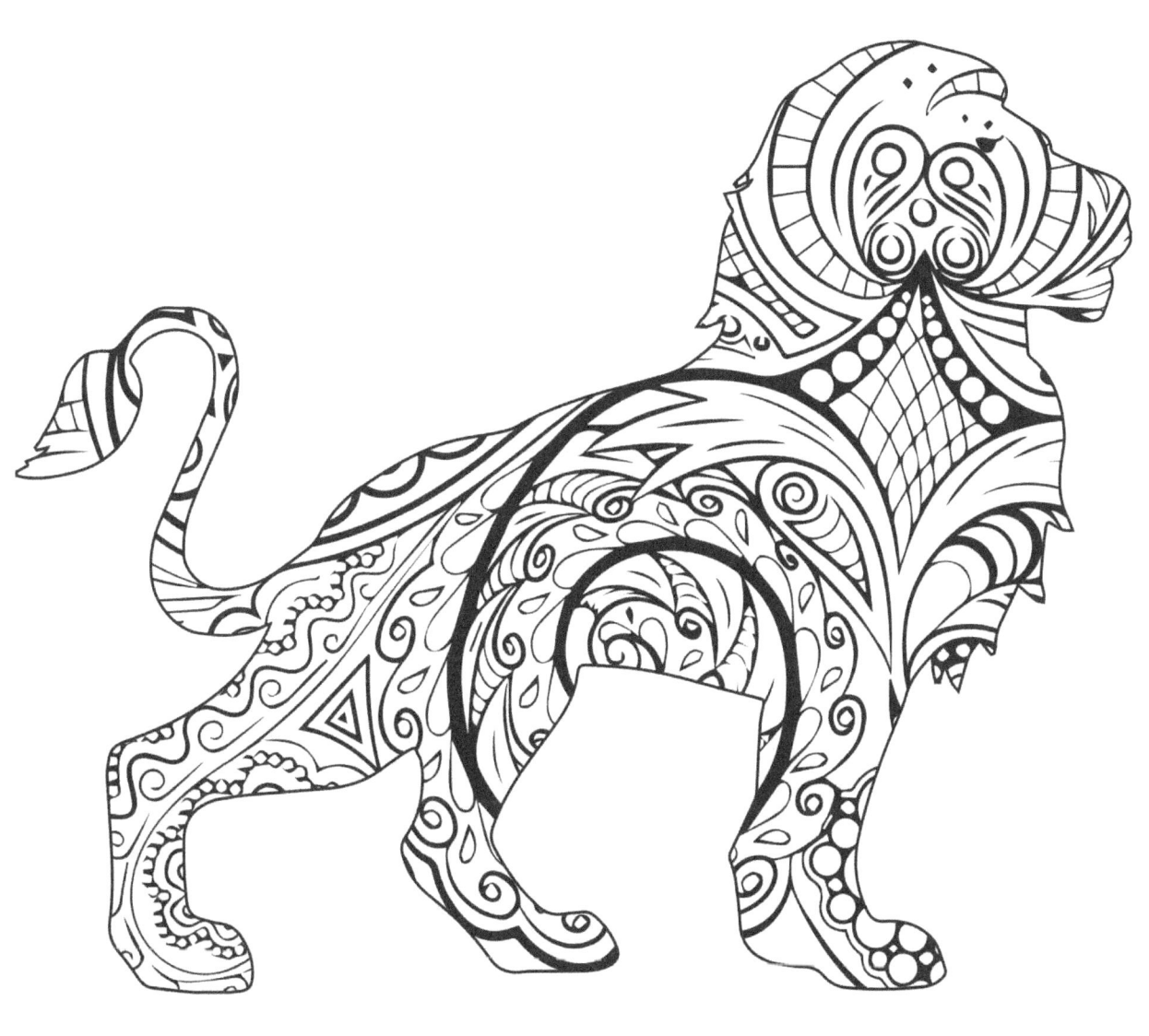

DIFFICULTY LEVEL: CHALLENGING

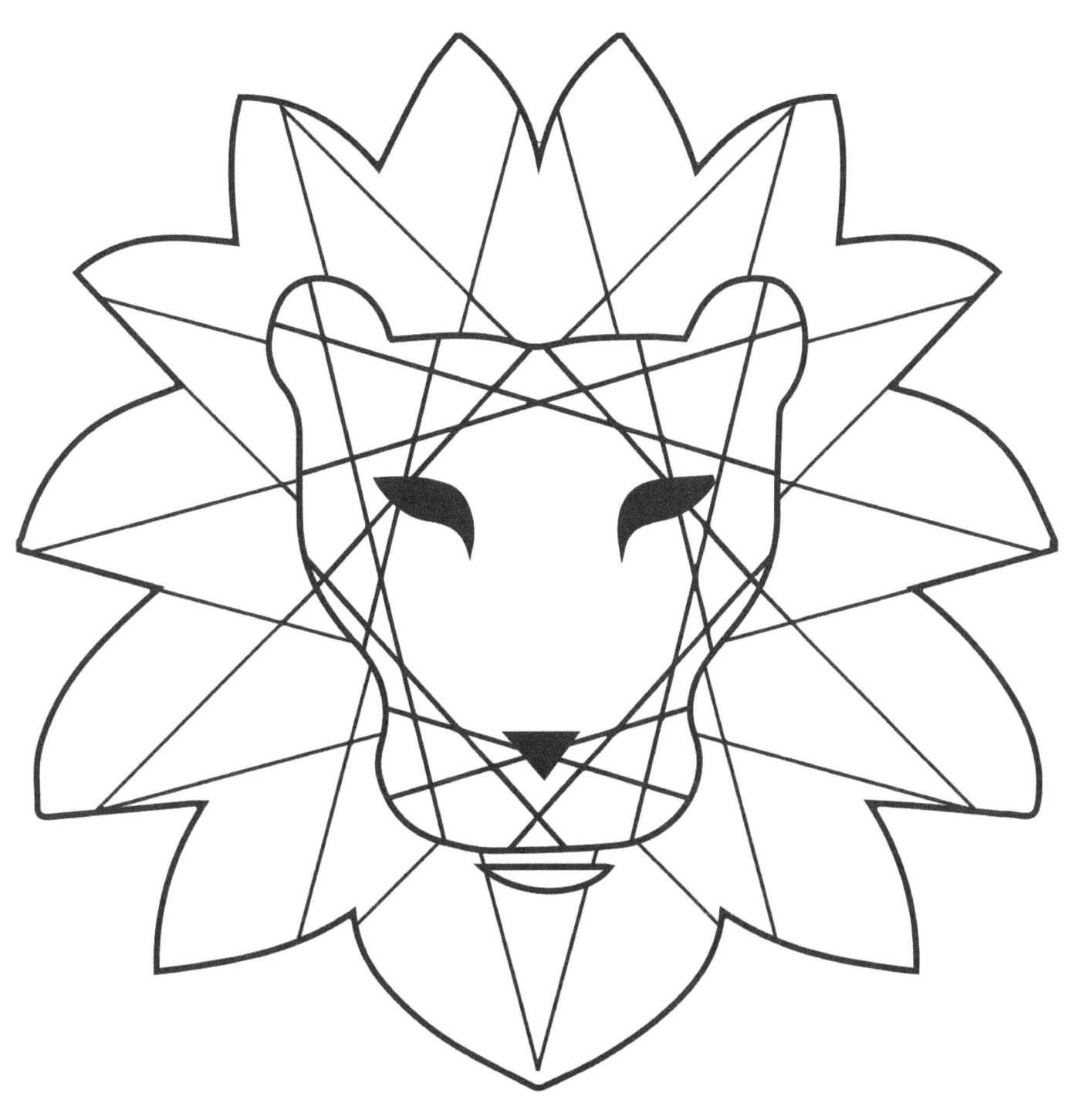

DIFFICULTY LEVEL: EASY

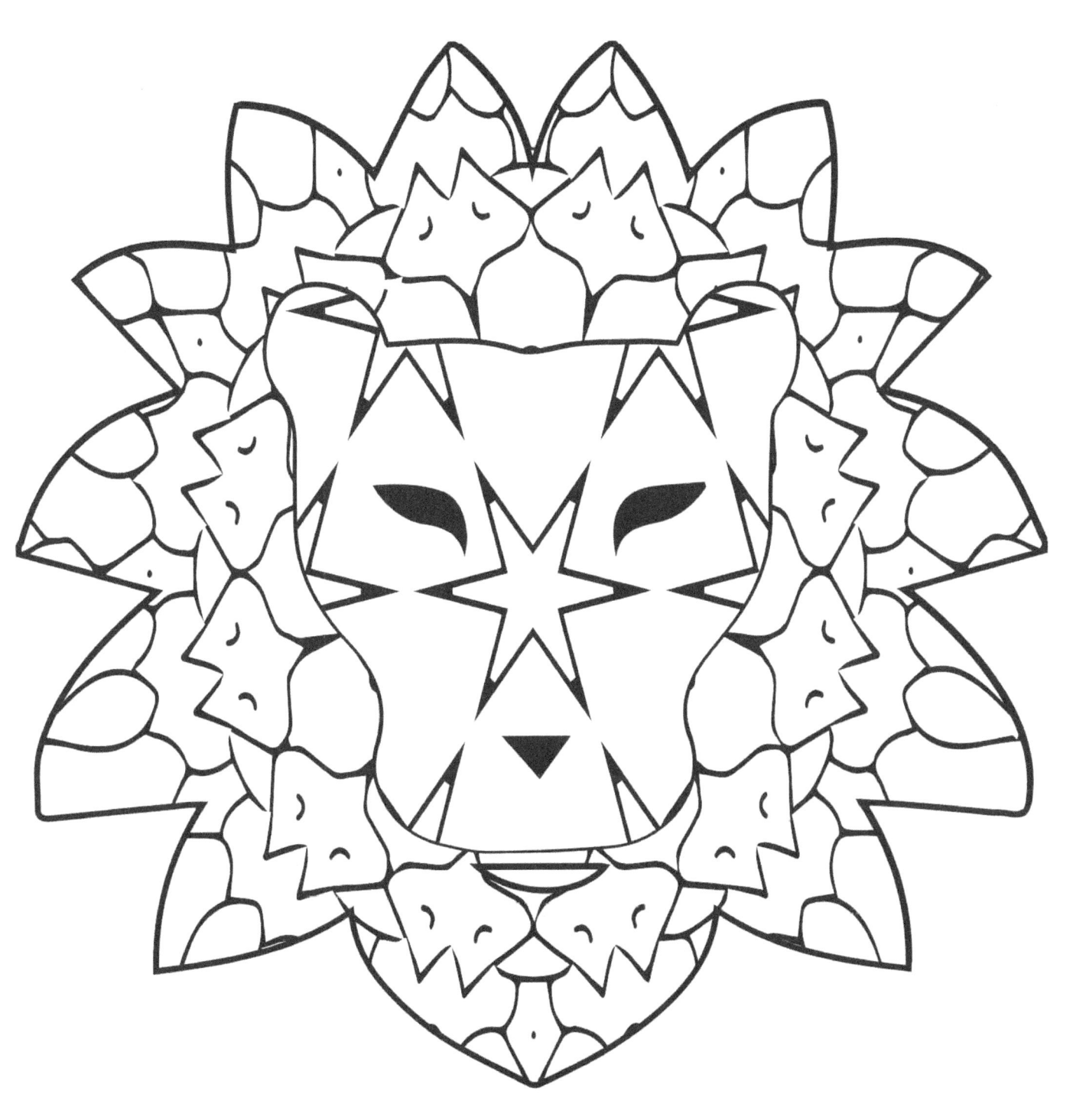

DIFFICULTY LEVEL: INTERMEDIATE

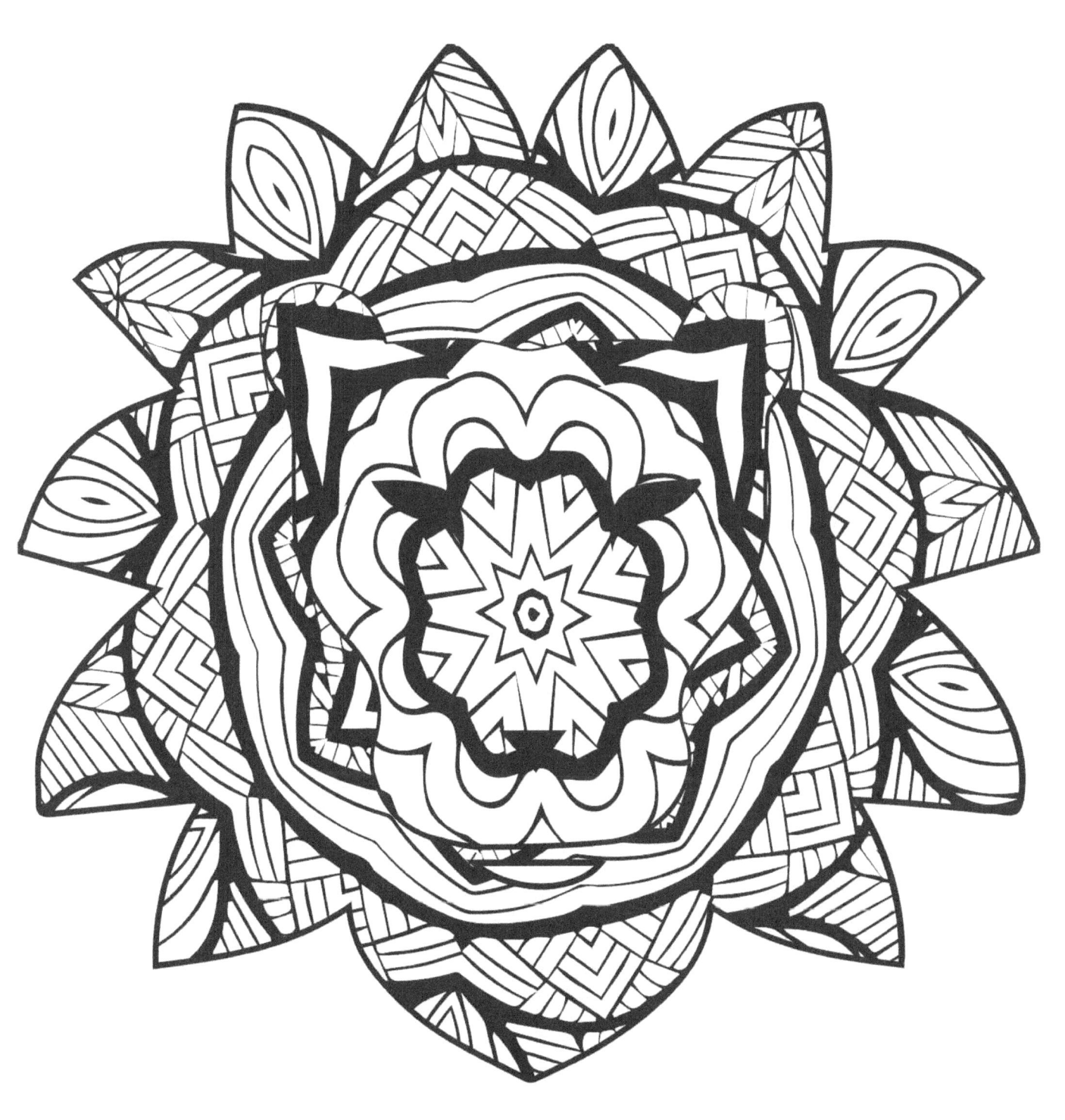

DIFFICULTY LEVEL: CHALLENGING

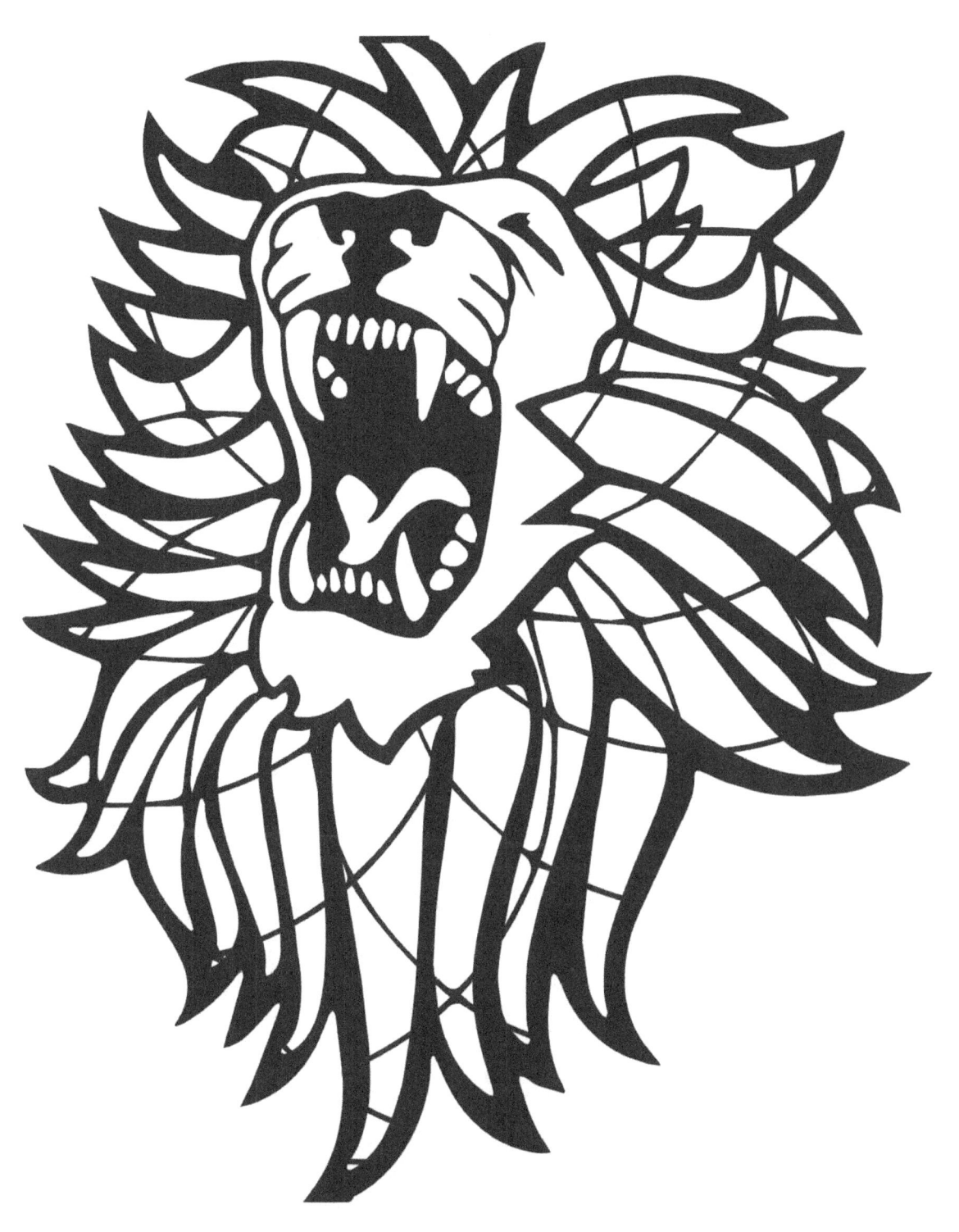

DIFFICULTY LEVEL: EASY

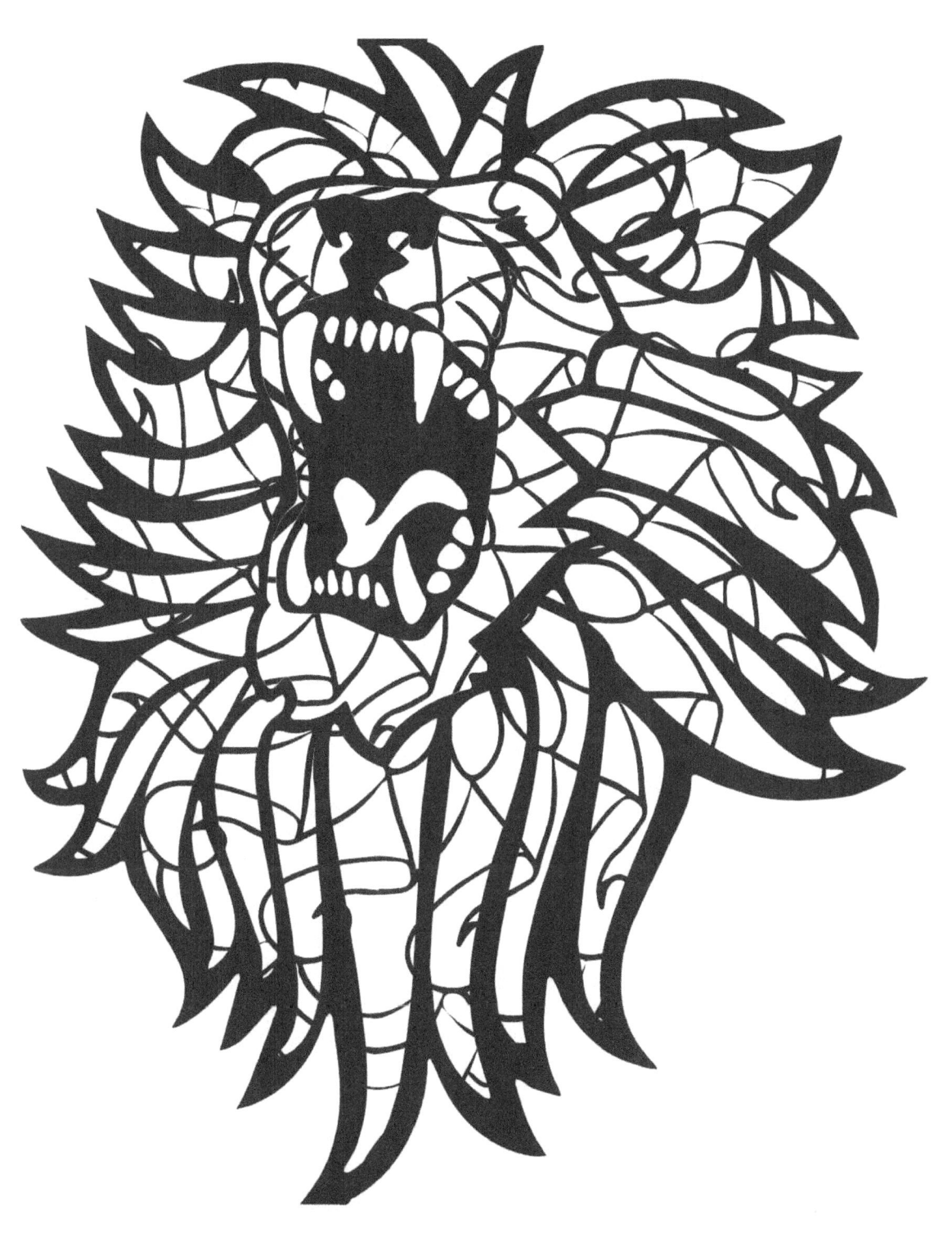

DIFFICULTY LEVEL: INTERMEDIATE

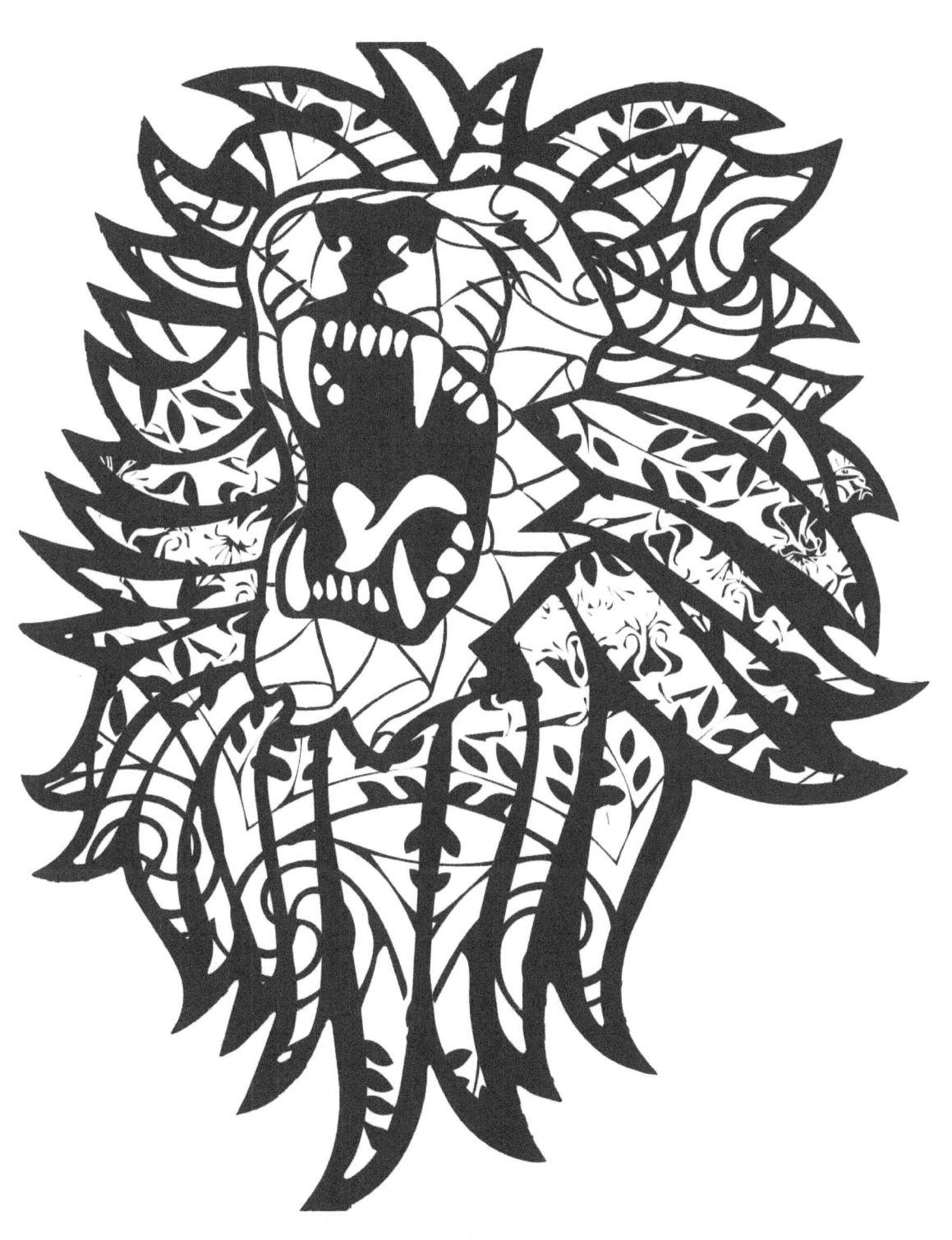

DIFFICULTY LEVEL: CHALLENGING

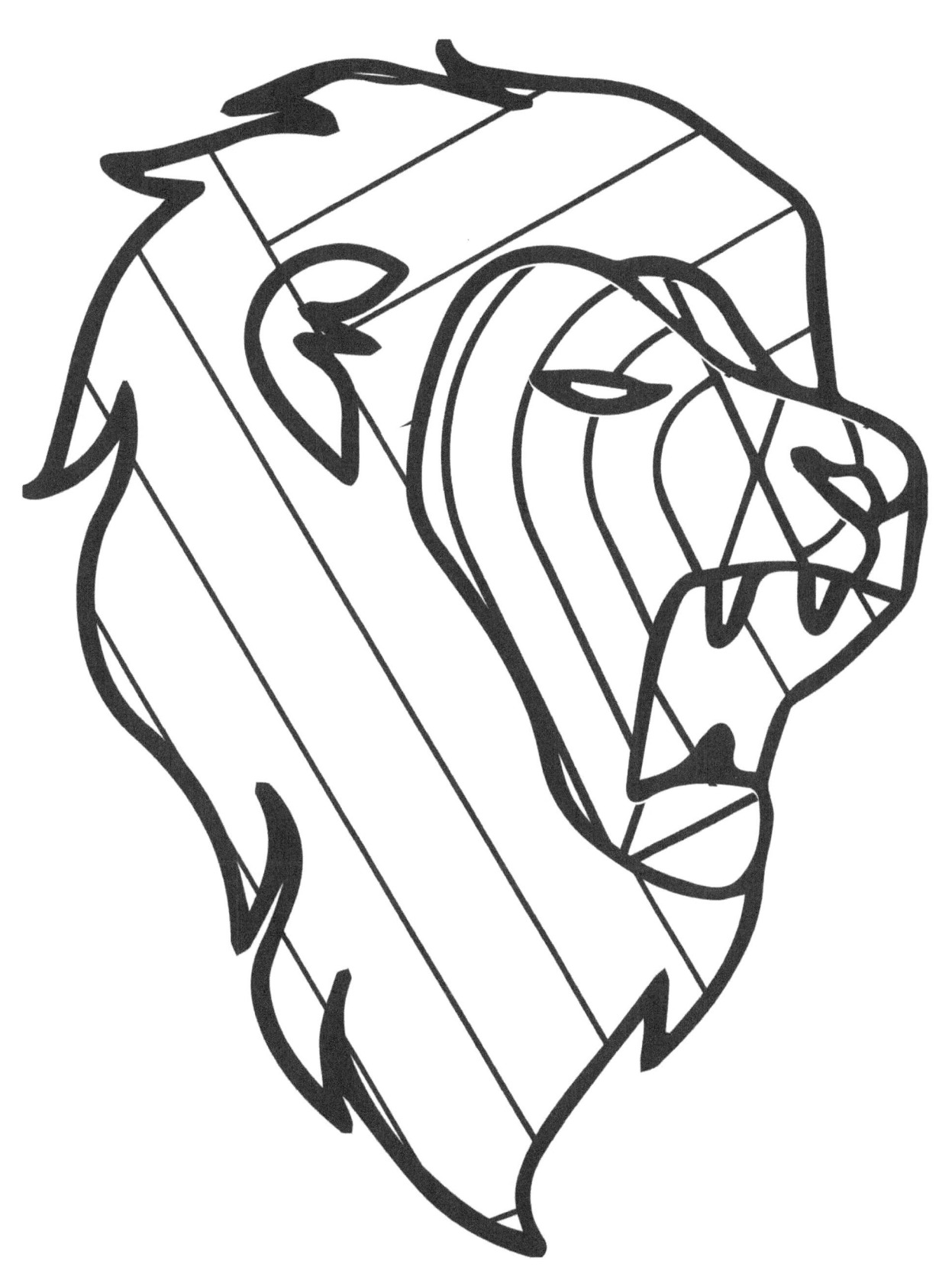

DIFFICULTY LEVEL: EASY

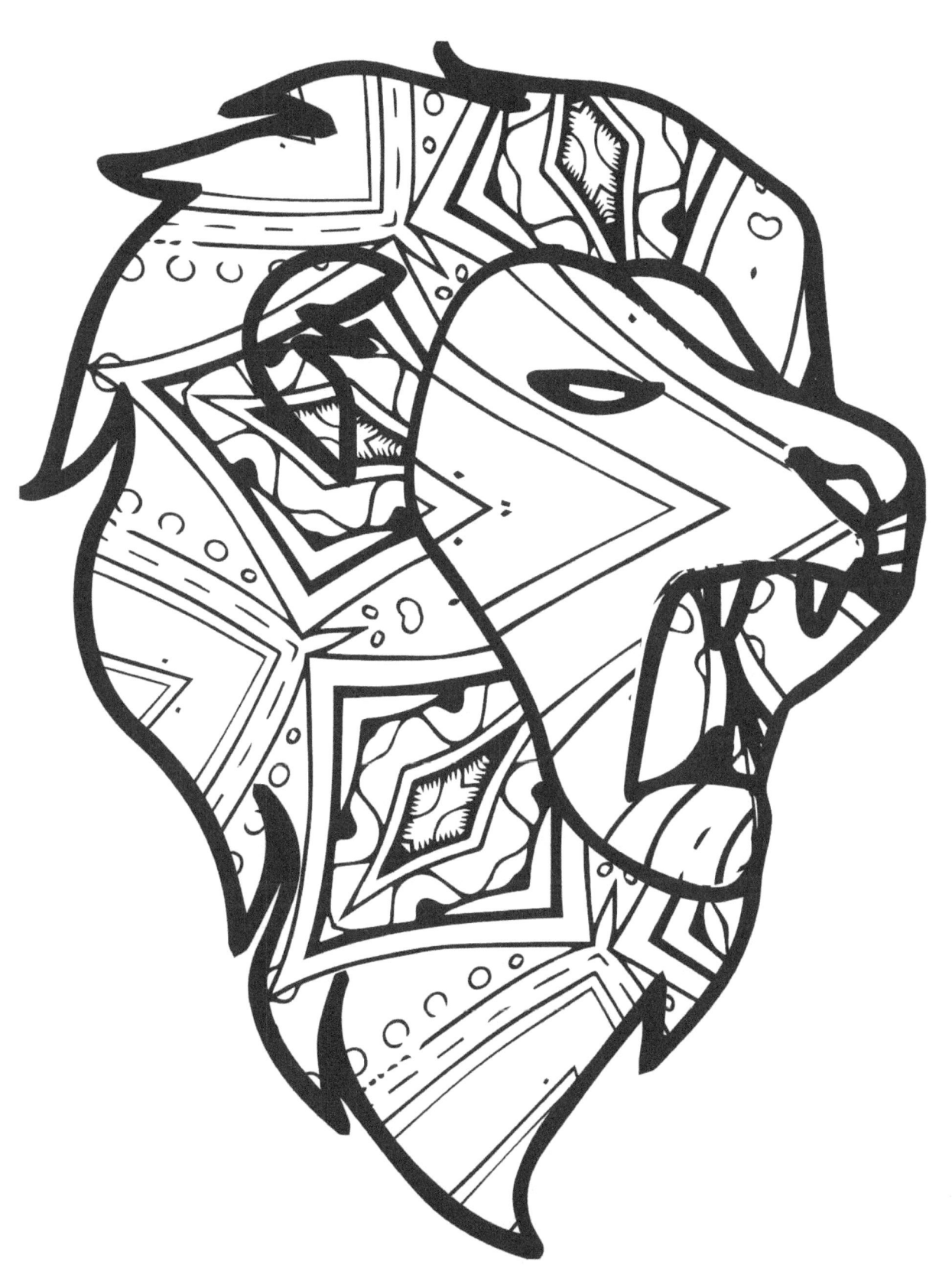

DIFFICULTY LEVEL: INTERMEDIATE

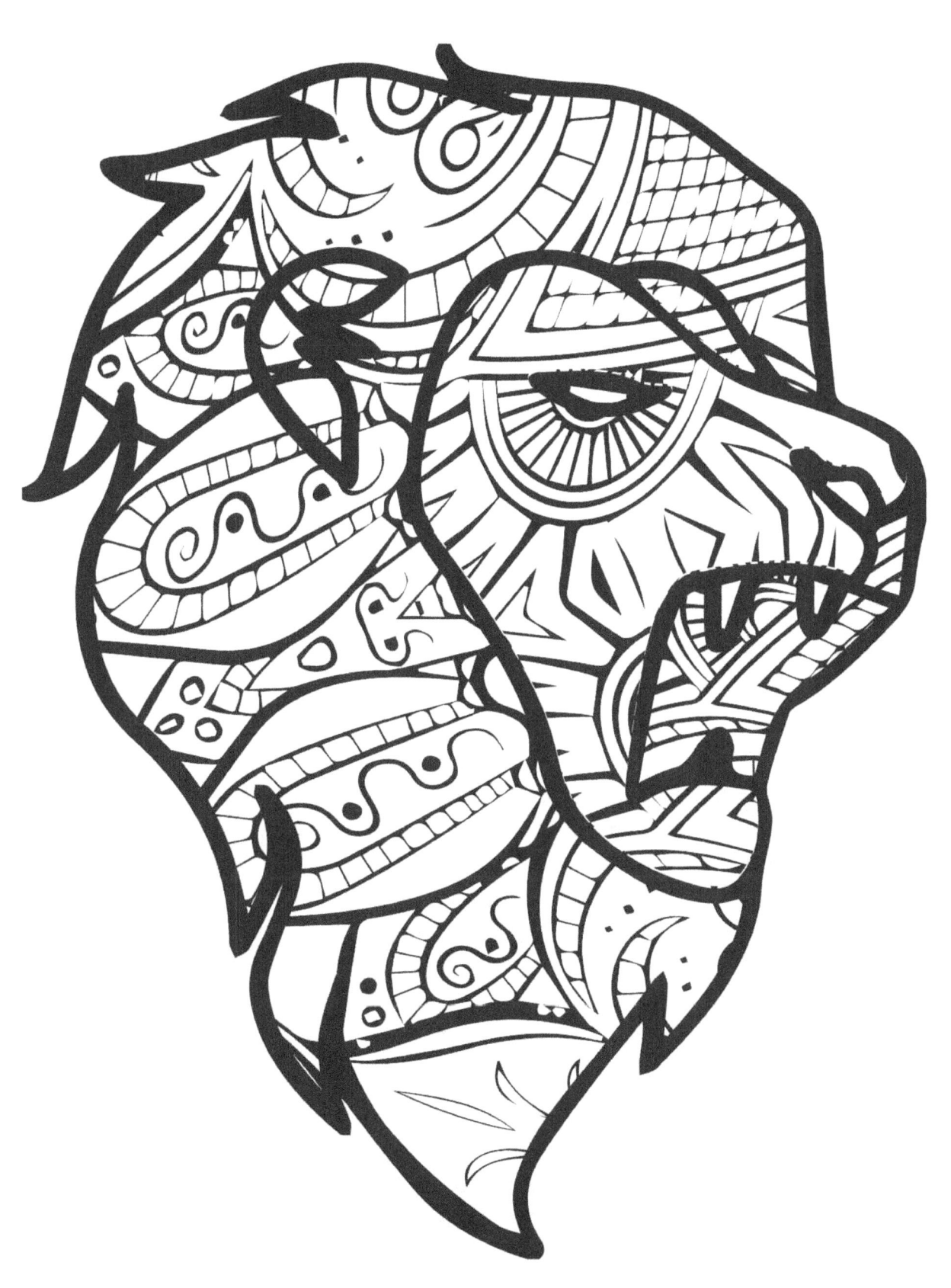

DIFFICULTY LEVEL: CHALLENGING

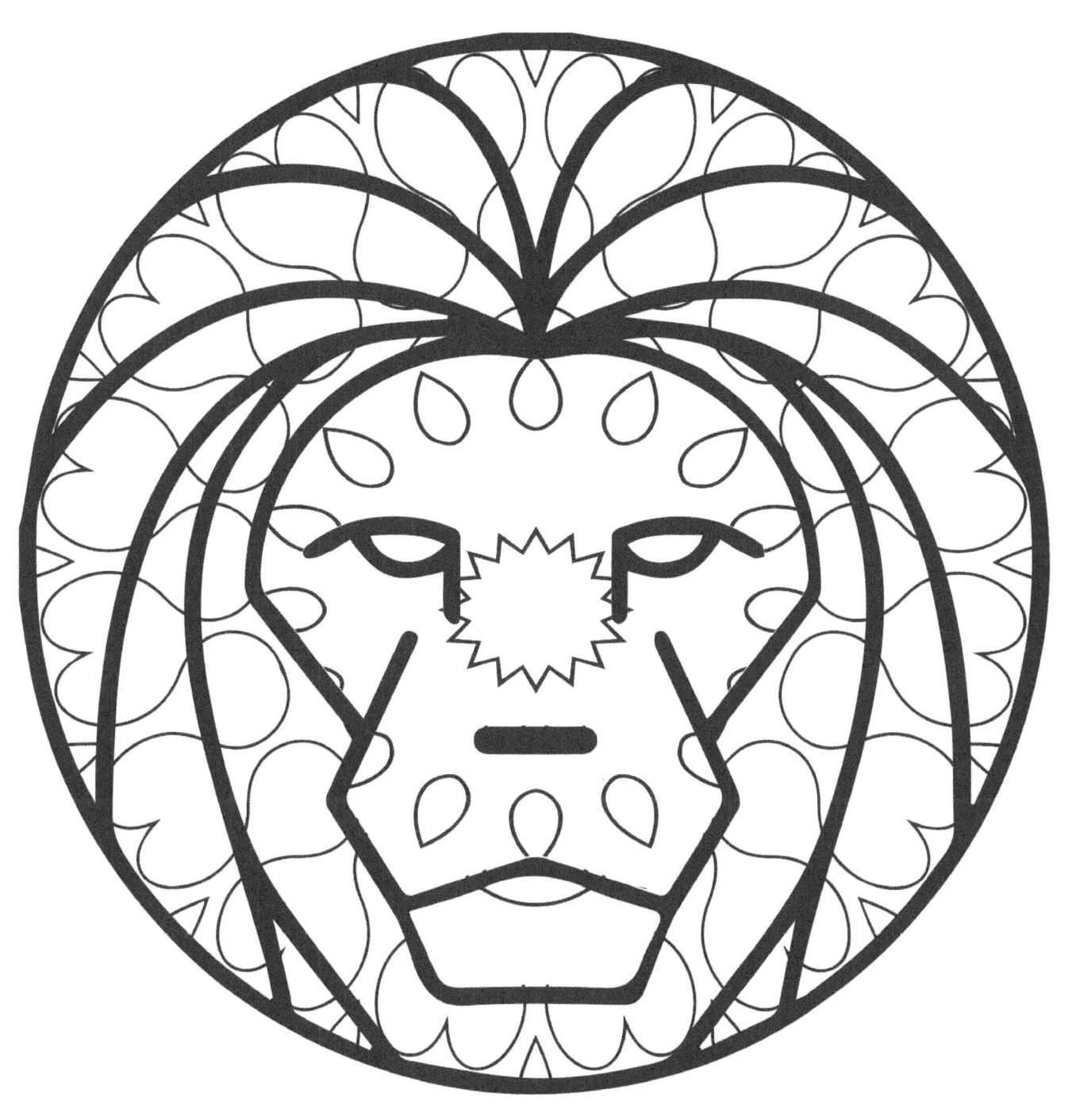

DIFFICULTY LEVEL: EASY

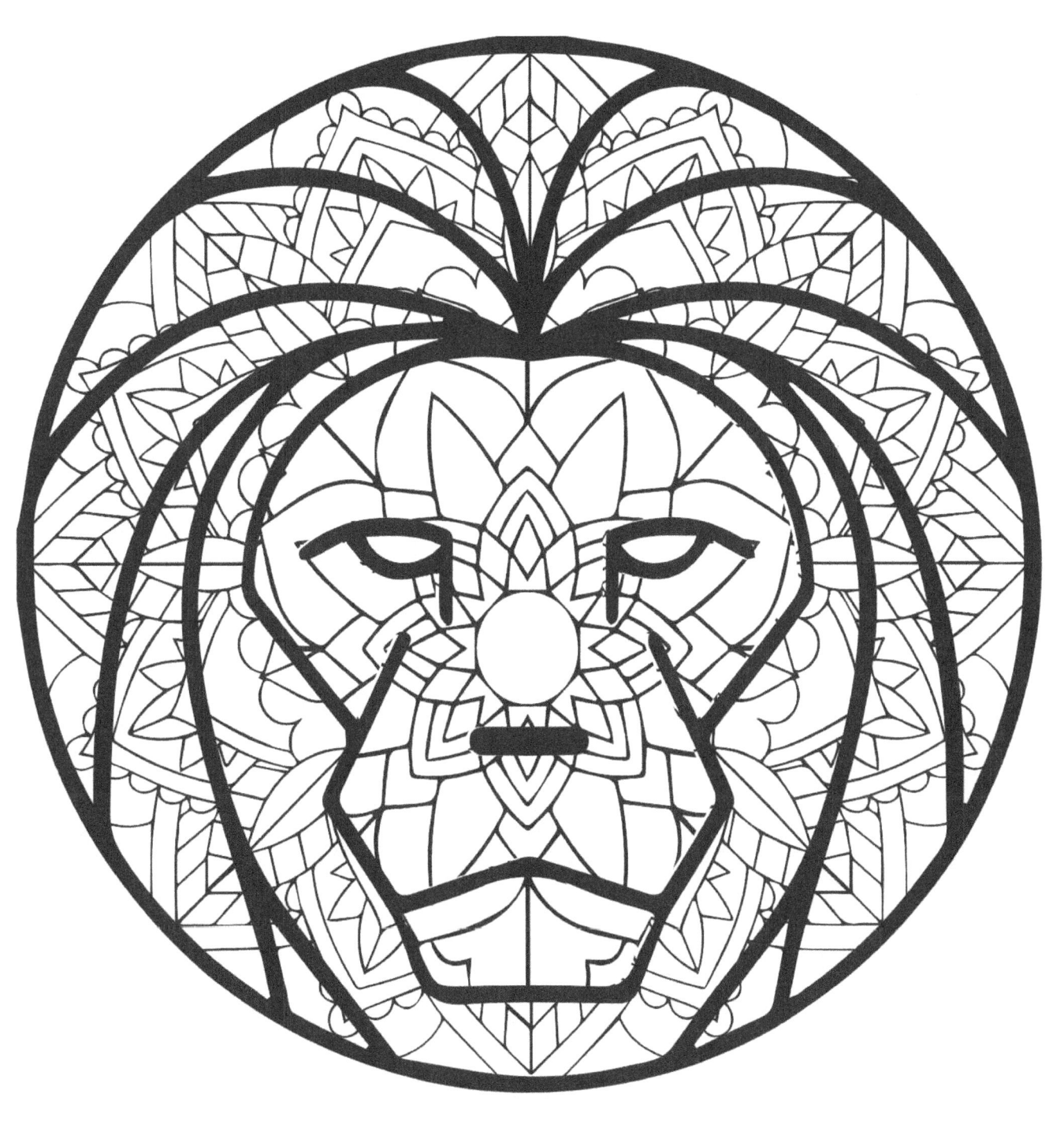

DIFFICULTY LEVEL: INTERMEDIATE

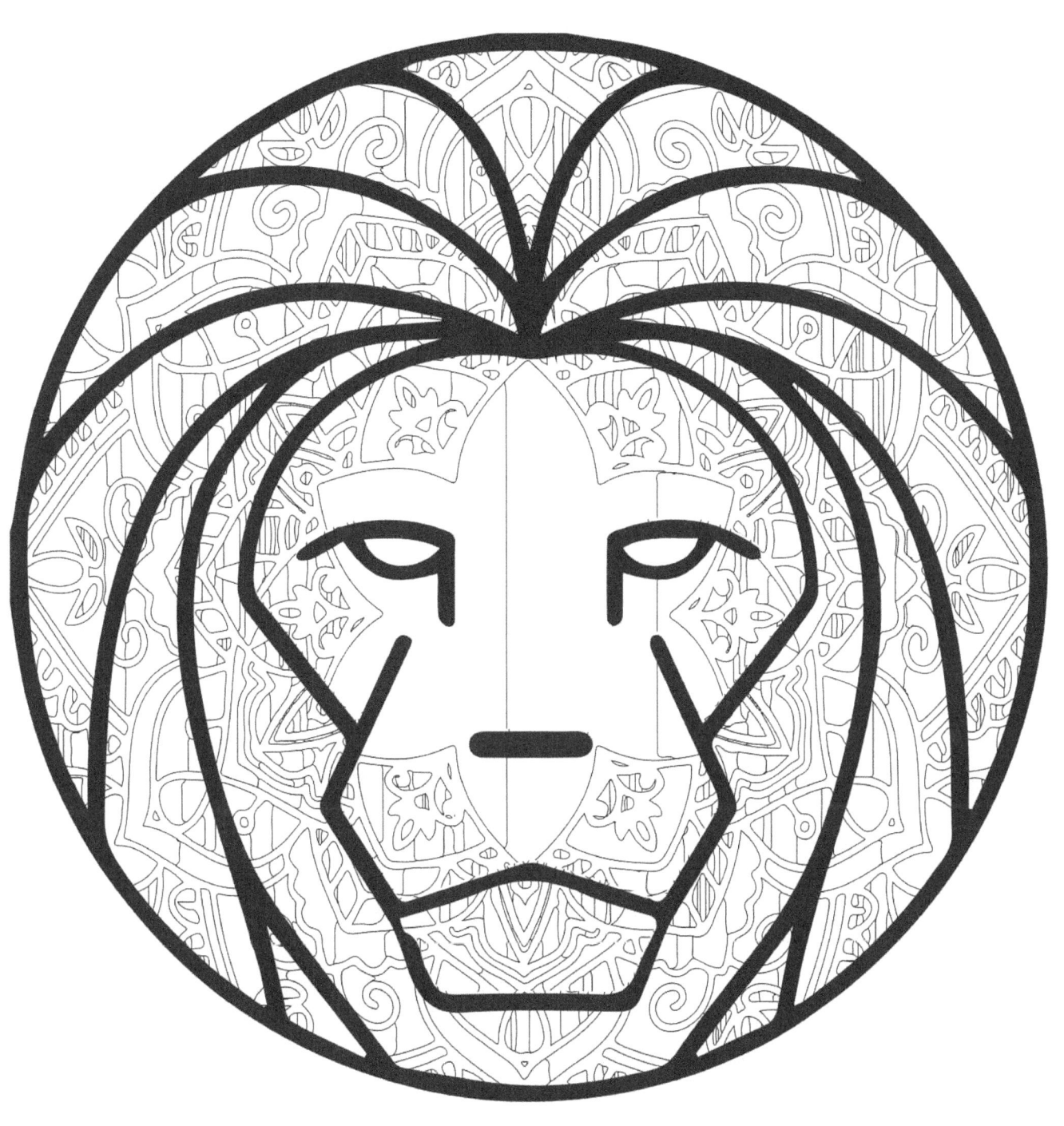

DIFFICULTY LEVEL: CHALLENGING

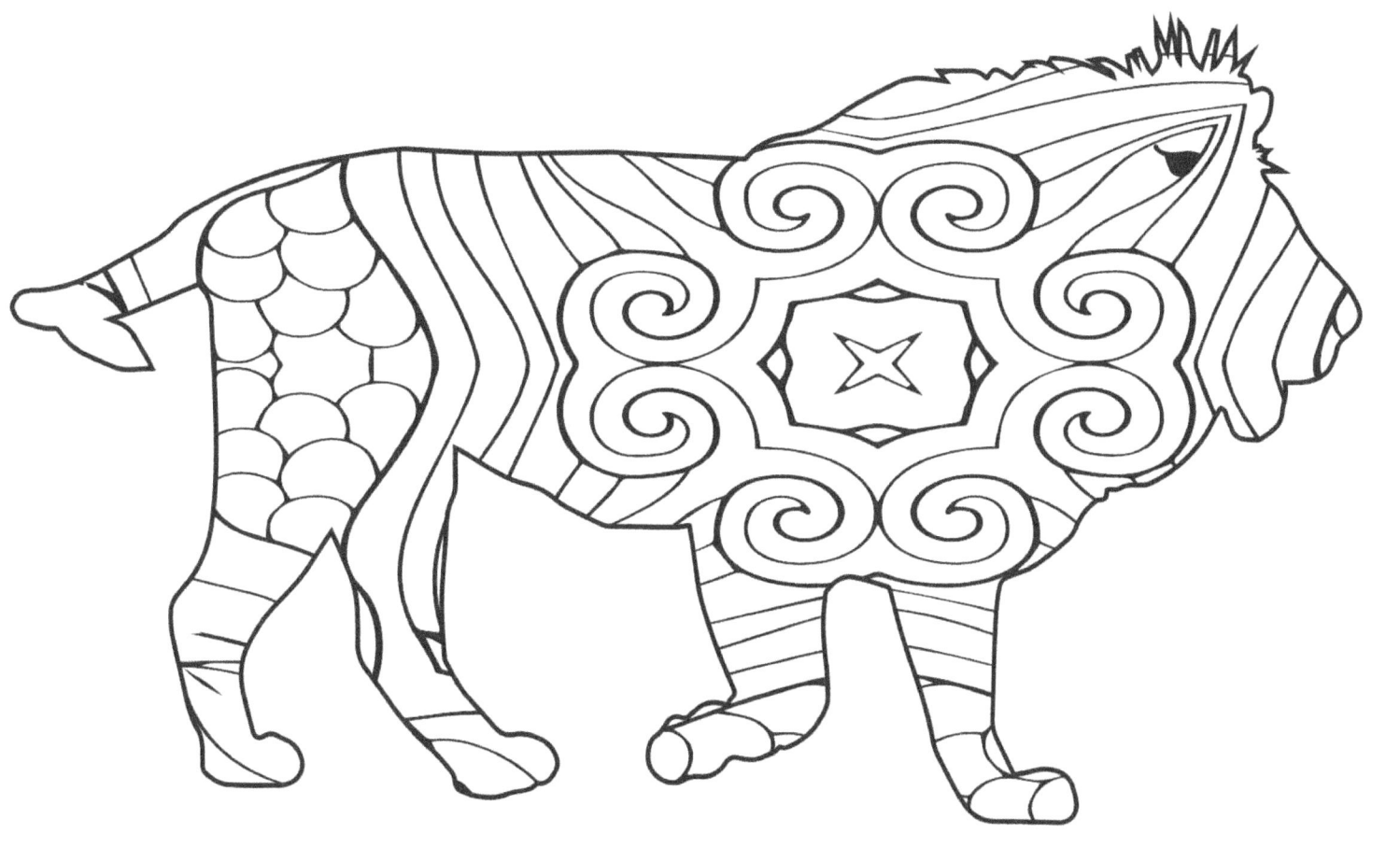

DIFFICULTY LEVEL: EASY

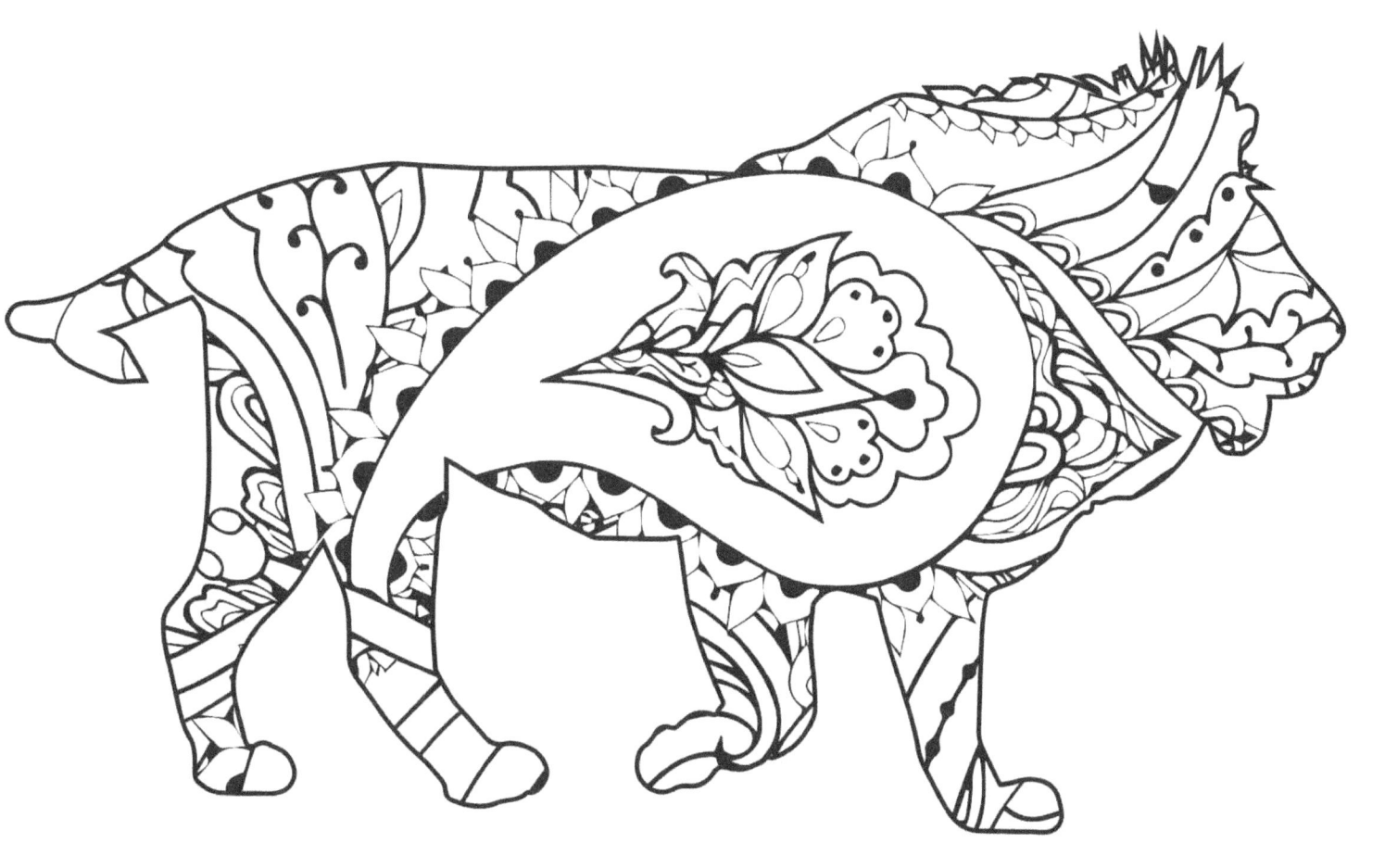

DIFFICULTY LEVEL: INTERMEDIATE

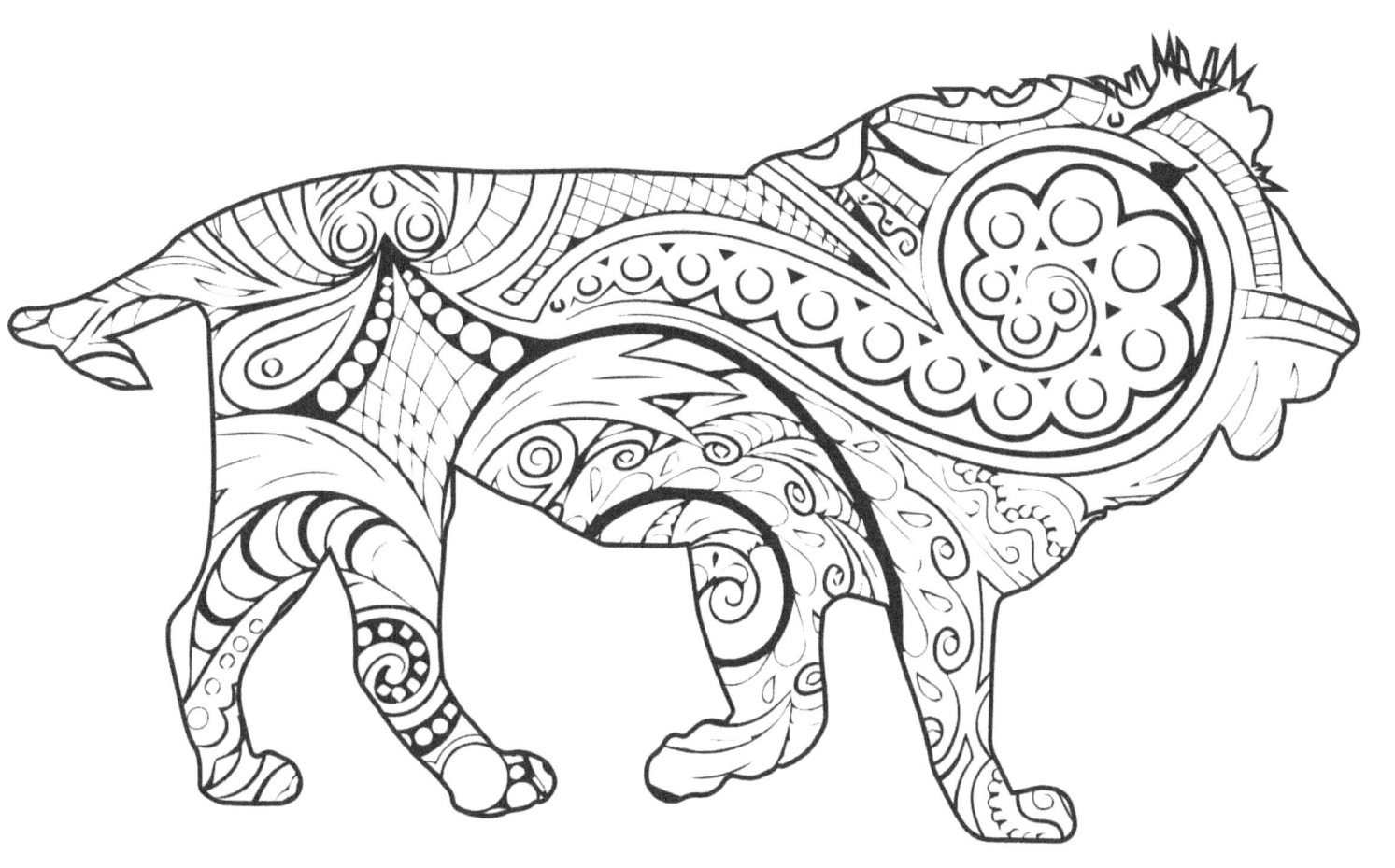

DIFFICULTY LEVEL: CHALLENGING

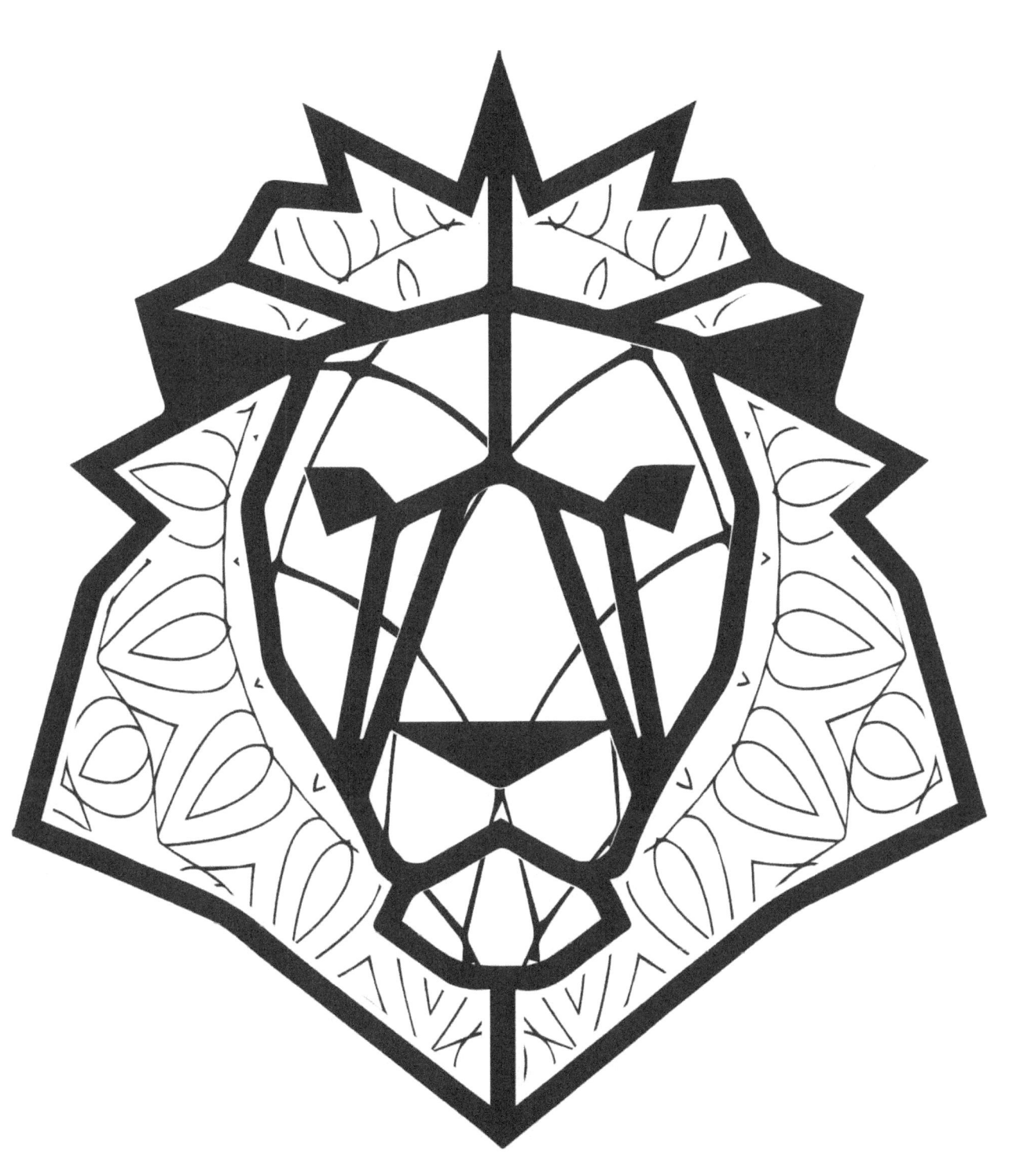

DIFFICULTY LEVEL: EASY

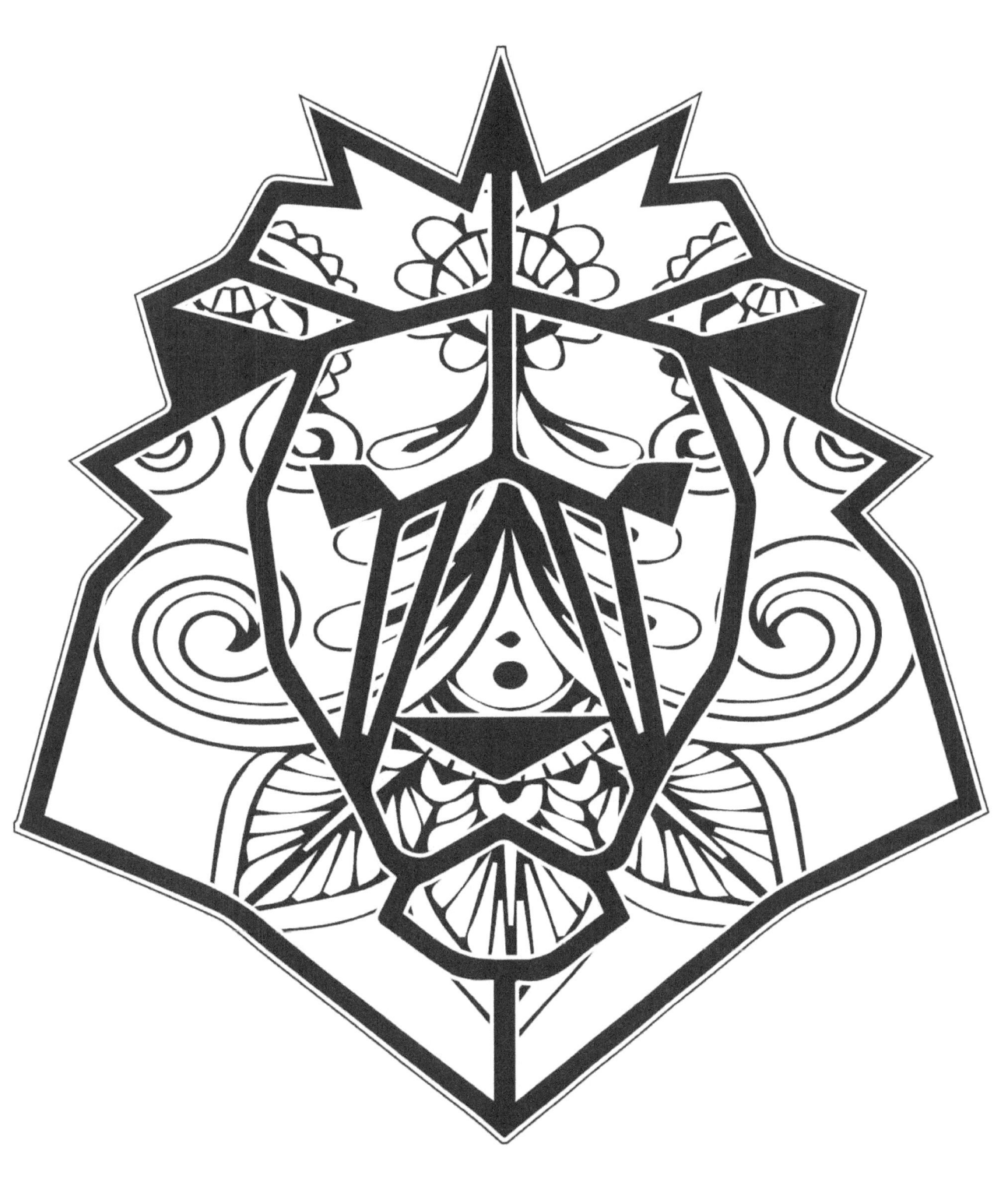

DIFFICULTY LEVEL: INTERMEDIATE

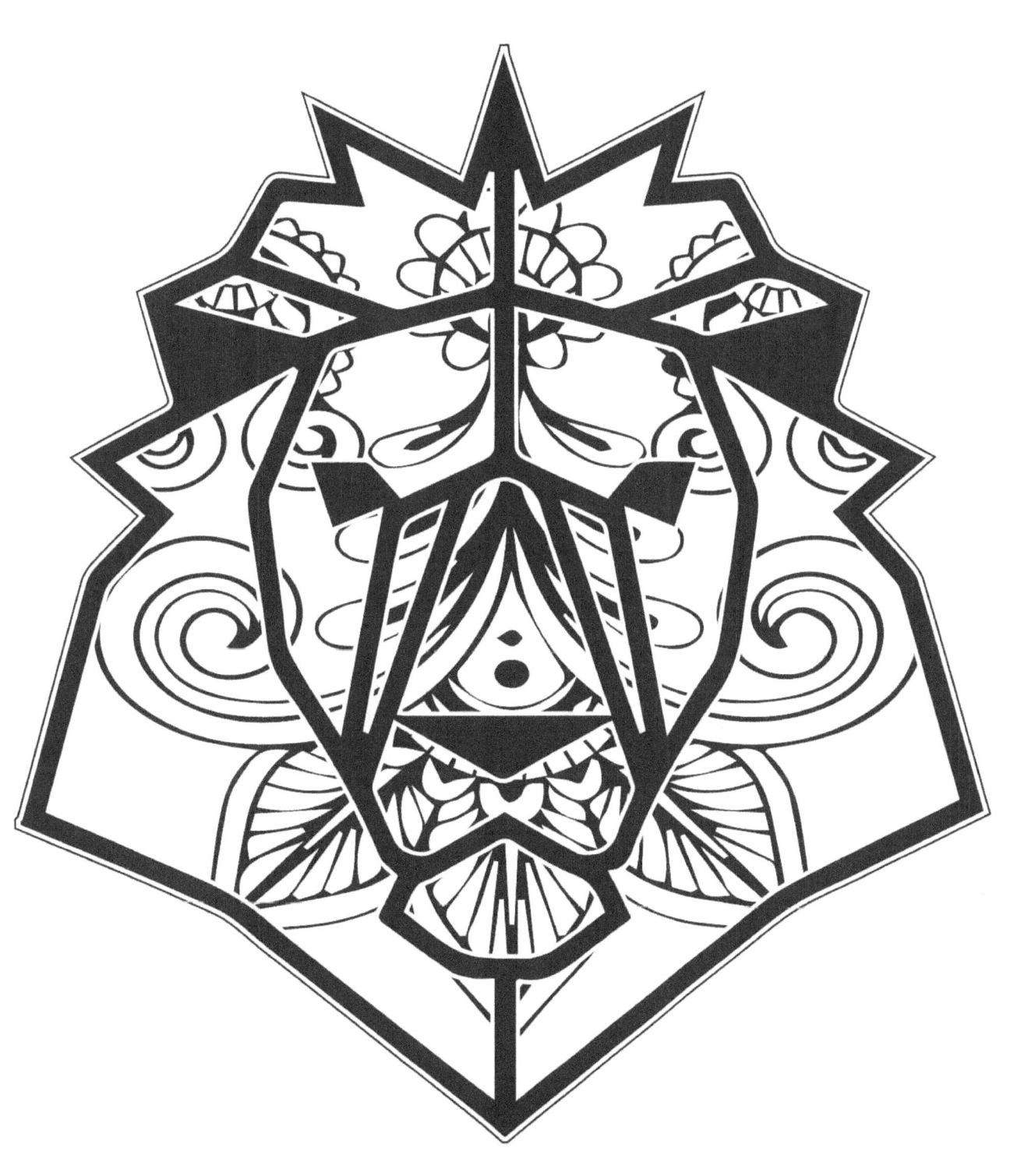

DIFFICULTY LEVEL: INTERMEDIATE

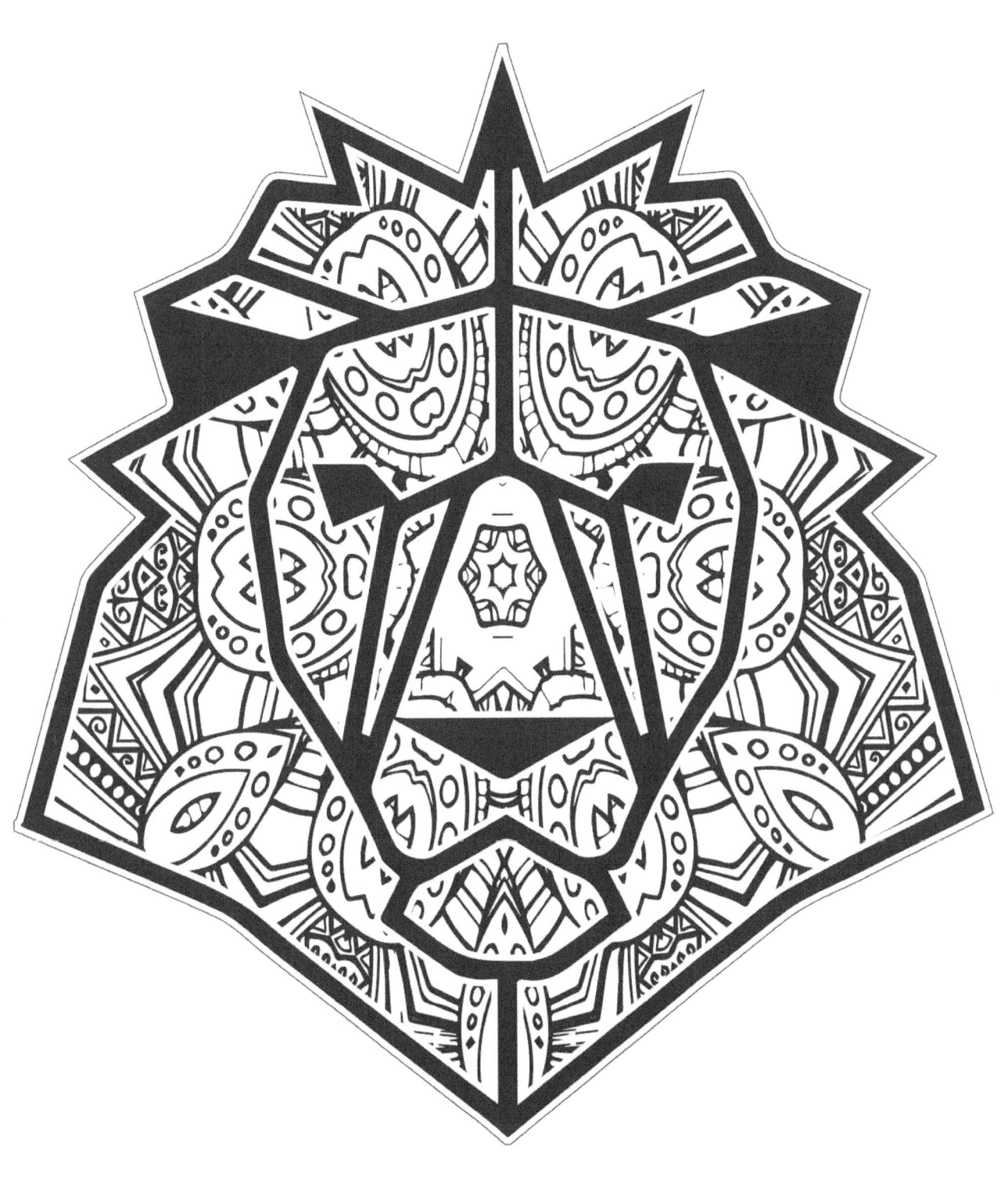

DIFFICULTY LEVEL: CHALLENGING

www.ingramcontent.com/pod-product-compliance
Lightning Source LLC
Chambersburg PA
CBHW080842220526
45467CB00008B/2357